"To Live, is to Love..."

THE E.Q. REVOLUTION
Envisioning a Brighter Future for Humanity

From

Emotional Intelligence

To

Emotional Maturity

The Best Strategies to Healing
the Most Important Relationship you
can ever Hope for, with *YOURSELF...*

Giving you the Tools you need to not only
Survive
in the New Era, but to Thrive in it!

MICHAEL VINCENT MOORE

THE E.Q. REVOLUTION
From Emotional Intelligence to Emotional Maturity

ISBN
978-1-989856-07-9 (Book)
978-1-989856-06-2 (E-book)

Elaquint Publishing

Cover background water image: by Max Ravier, on Pexels

Thank you for purchasing this book

Personal disclaimer: Emotional maturity and finding purpose and meaning in life is an immense field to get into, one which no one has all the answers to. So understand that I am speaking from my experiences and the vast and varied research and studies I have undertaken. That it all makes sense to me doesn't mean I claim any of this as the absolute truth, and really, is there such a thing anyway? It is not a research paper nor thesis, it is a book meant to help people advance to a greater life, that dares to expand on our current models, and I hope I have managed to do a good job of it. I highly encourage people to seek their own truths wherever those truths may be found, and to not hang on too tightly to anything any one person or group might say.

Dedicated to *Everyone*

Thanks for your interest, I hope you enjoy the read!

PLEASE LEAVE A REVIEW: If you appreciate the book and its message, please leave a review on Amazon, or wherever you have purchased the book from. Not only is the gesture greatly appreciated, but it helps to continue spreading the positive message that this book (and the whole project) intends to communicate. You can also share with your own network as well, or post in your social media presence. Without reviews and positive encouragements, works today have a hard time making it through, and since it is meant to better individuals and humanity, what healthier way to become part of the message, than to become one yourself?

You can also get in touch if you are working in a related field and believe that we can help each other expand our understanding and reach in regards to making this place of ours even better...

And also, get involved in a great cause, if not this one, find another, or create one of your own!

Table of Contents

A note to readers

Life seems to be becoming progressively challenging, not just in regards to finding a proper career path, excelling in our chosen field, having a salary that is not only equivalent to our skills and expectations but which we can actually have a decent life on, pay increasingly expensive rents and mortgages while wondering if our medical expenses and retirement will be taken care of. But also in all the additional things we need to keep in mind; politics, social engagement, complicated utilities and communications, privacy, and all sorts of other time consuming concerns, even global pandemics, all requiring our time and effort to keep up with. And those are just some of the details we need to contend with on a daily basis. But what about us, our deeper sense of self, love, happiness, when can we be enough at peace with what we are doing, with our whole environment, to have time to get back to basics, the most important things in our lives that can provide us with a sense of accomplishment and harmony?

We are being increasingly conditioned into believing that finding our place in this world is about things that are outside of us. We need to take a step back and rethink what we've been made to accept as important in life. It is time to get back to us, what is most important in *our* lives. To perform a deep reset of all of our internal systems, to let go of dysfunctional conditioning that keeps leading us down dead end roads, fruitless endeavors, away from true love and togetherness.

There is a growing body of evidence demonstrating that this "better path" starts with developing **Emotional Intelligence**, and I say we need to go beyond that, and develop **Emotional Maturity.** That distinction, and how to go about it, is the main focus of this book.

It is a well-timed excursion into what it truly means to be human in today's world, and also, it is a work in progress, as we all are.

Here are some of the main topics elaborated throughout these pages:

- How developing emotional maturity relates to self-love, and how that relates to having your sense of belonging and self-worth come from deep within you
- Seeing and feeling the world through the "eyes" of your heart, to be real, to *do* you
- Resetting all of your energy systems so that they can work better together, reducing dysfunctional programming and conditioning
- The evils of narcissism, and how to root it out of your life
- The greater need for sensitive people to develop emotional maturity, to understand themselves better, for the world to make sense to them, and learn how to stand strong within insensitive environments
- Developing intelligent boundaries and finding your tribe
- Healing of past wounds, and present day relationships with others and yourself
- Understanding how we spend our lives running away from the things we do not face within ourselves, and to stop being victims of our emotions.
- Learning a communal language, a new vocabulary that your whole being can understand; mind and emotions, body and brain, feelings, memories, past and future, all coalescing into expressing yourself back into full present awareness
- How changing yourself is changing the world, playing your part in the big picture towards a new era for humankind, and the extent to which the future of humanity depends on how many people are willing to undertake this path of change

"Each of us must work for his own improvement, and at the same time share a general responsibility for all humanity..."
– Marie Curie

That said and done, now off to the intro!

Introduction

Toot! Toot! Toot!

That is my impression of a bugle.

So, what for you may ask?

A call to arms!

Not of the old, not of weapons nor conflicts, but to deeper motives and higher aspirations.

To do what we must to not leave our fate to chance, to ensure that humanity is steered towards a **thriving future**, instead of merely surviving our times. To march on into the next era of our evolution, to set our steps to aims of greater purpose.

So, a call to love, a call to inspire, a call to go where no human has gone before... Okay, that's a bit over the top. But there is a point in there, that last reference was to *Star Trek*, and although fiction, the creators of the show did paint a pretty picture in regards to what kind of future holds promise in regards to nearly ending much of the problems we currently face in our societies, and how humanity had joined together to achieve greater aspirations.

To come back to us, what exactly can we do, like, right now, to start working on that kind of idyllic future?

Who *exactly* knows, maybe that is why many don't bother much with it in the first place. But to do nothing is to accept all the ills of our current society, and when you start looking, you'll find much more than you might care to see. Many believe we are declining as a race, even though we are advancing from a technological point of view, within ourselves, and as a whole, we don't seem to be getting anywhere near peace on a global scale; poverty, disease, wars, conflicts, materialism, terrorism, abuse, corruption... Those are all very strong indicators when considering if a species is thriving or not, and we wouldn't score very high on those markers if some alien race would put us through a galactic trial on higher morals and intents.

I'm not one to stand on the sidelines waiting for someone else to come up with a better plan. Not to say that my plan is perfect, but I'm convinced it can help. And I believe it starts with developing into **Emotional Maturity** on a grand scale, starting with every single individual.

But, this is much more than your standard manual for learning about *emotional intelligence*...

First, to understand that most of us seek the same things in life, that we are much more united at our deepest level than we realize, where it counts most. Whether the pursuit of lasting happiness, the exploration of our inner selves, of our soul, unconditional love, of a higher reality, of God, community, a spiritual enlightened path, emotional and psychological healing, communing with an eternal/collective consciousness, belief systems and religions, emotional intelligence, soul mates, living in the present moment, purpose and meaning... Yes, that's a long list, and it *all* comes down to pretty much the same thing, a better understanding of what it is to be human, to overcome our past, understanding our emotions and feelings for us not to be a hostage to them, and instead find a truer expression of our deeper selves, a deeper connection to our reality.

"My mission in life is not merely to survive, but to thrive; and to do so with some passion, some compassion, some humor, and some style..." – **Maya Angelou**

Introduction

To master our pain and suffering, to free ourselves from the effects of all of our past mistakes, hurts experienced, and regrets. To feel alive in full, aware of who we are and what we want out of life, and not just of simple goals that keep us moving in a forward momentum, but to feel that we are not compromising any of our values, and that we are not abandoning any of our self along that road. And to feel that we are each living up to our maximum ability, to our highest expectations of ourselves, and not the expectations of others or of society.

Isn't that what we all seek, the truths that we all have in common?

The desire that people have of changing the world, not just leaving their mark, but of having a positive contribution that will last, that will endure the times. What better way than to love, and share that love, and help people change within themselves. And with that change, they become free to pursue their own path of meaning, regardless of what they will end up doing, as long as their balance of self-love has been increased, then everything they do will be based on an increase of love and compassion.

How can anyone go wrong following such a path?

Then whatever you do will not be so important, the details will work themselves out, as long as the foundation is strong, and based on loving and compassionate feelings. Fears come and go, as with anger and jealousy, but love withstands, it edifies, it goes beyond the ephemeral nature of matter and attachments. The tallest structures on Earth, regardless of the ingenuity and skills involved to make them, all will crumble eventually, all will return to dust, only to be replaced by some other "grand" accomplishment. But who we are at the end of the day, when all has come and gone, when we lay our head on our pillows and surrender ourselves to sleep, that is who we will wake up in the morning with, and that will never change until death do you part. And the impact of who we are, if we are so fortunate as to have an impact, a good one, that is the only thing that truly counts. That is the hope that drives our deepest wishes, underneath all selfish motives, fears and unreconciled past.

Who are You, and what do *You* really want out of Life?

Do you know, or are you just moving from one moment to the other, hoping it'll just come to you one day, that by some miracle, your life will make sense, and all the pieces will fall together, nicely aligned...

Developing Emotional Maturity might not be the cure all of your worries, to bring about the manifestation of all of your dreams, but it is the only place to get a good start of things. Otherwise your life will always be controlled by the emotions and fears you have not yet been able to understand, that greatly diminish your existence. That might be the greatest struggle of humanity, not climate problems, not technology, or how we will build a community on Mars, nothing to do about our dominance over any planet or solar system, but the mastery of our own internal selves.

I use various techniques in this book, from enlightened quotes, music, humor, exercises, mindful observation techniques, and even a bit of poking, all in the hopes of instilling some kind of awareness to our greater journey in life, the one beyond what our eyes can see. To know that **we are not alone in our suffering**, that we are all connected in our struggles, if only we can grow a bit of courage and let those things out of our system, and to know how to get there.

2020 has been a tough year in so many ways, and people need hope, and not just hope, but to feel that that hope is within their grasp. The illusions that things will just work out on their own, or that there will always be "someone" to come to our rescue are wearing thin. We need to find a way to empower ourselves for the years to come, and not contenting ourselves with merely coasting by, or relying on systems and authority figures to get to our better future. Not to fight against anything specifically, but to take the fight within ourselves, to free our own self from the things that keep us grounded or drifting in autopilot. If there is one thing the current pandemic has taught us, is that there is no magic solution other than to make sure we ourselves are in top "operating" mode, not just free of this new virus (or developing anti-bodies), but emotionally, physically, and psychologically sound, the **masters of our own domains**.

Greatness, Love and Happiness, let no one deprive you from them, and for that, you must make yourself as free from unhealthy elements within yourself as you can.

"The only journey is the one within..."
– Rainer Maria Rilke

You, me, everyone, we have so much in common with our journey, our deepest aspirations, at least the most important aspects of it. But we so often let the little details come in between us, to keep us in misery, to make our lives mundane and isolated, and keeping our world in conflict and strife. Then the search for temporary distractions and short term goals ends up consuming most of our waking hours... Well, I don't want to get too much into this in the introduction as that is what this book is about, so then some might think they don't need to bother reading on, and you'll end up missing out on great things because I gave up too much in the intro, like the next section on **how great your life can get if only you took the time to fine tune your emotional system**, and a few empowering words from Krishnamurti to kick things off...

PART 1: A Journey to Emotional Maturity, a New Era to Unfold...

"Revolution must begin with you and me. All great things start on a small scale, all great movements begin with individuals; and if we wait for collective action, such action, if it takes place at all, is destructive and conducive to further misery.

That revolution, that individual transformation, can take place only when we understand relationship, which is the process of self-knowledge. Without knowing the whole process of my relationship at all the different levels, what I think and what I do has no value at all. What basis have I for thinking if I do not know myself? We are so desirous to act, so eager to do something, to bring some kind of revolution, some kind of amelioration.

Real revolution does not come merely at the superficial level, at the economic level. Real revolution lies in our hearts and minds, and it can only come when we understand the whole total process of our being from day to day, in every relationship. And then only is there a possibility of preventing technical knowledge being used for the destruction of man.

We seem to forget that the world problem is the individual problem, that the problems of the world are created by you and me as individuals. The problems of war, starvation, exploitation, and all the other innumerable problems that confront each one of us are created by you and me, and as long as we do not understand ourselves at every level, we will maintain the rottenness of the present society."

– Jiddu Krishnamurti

To Believe in Something Great Again...

"Emotional immaturity is searching for love outside you. Emotional maturity comes from realizing you are the source of love..." – **Collette O'Mahony**

How Great do you Believe your Life can get?

Really, if you dared to dream, to let go, and not the childish dreams of wanting to become rich and famous without even knowing what that entails. I mean the really good dreams, the important ones, along the lines of curing cancer, building a homeless shelter or a school for children in a country where education is sparse, inventing a device to clean up the oceans, or even just basic dreams such as having a very loving relationship, in a relaxing kind of environment, good friends and such. Purpose and meaning, deep connections rather than luxury and wealth, that is what people wish for when they figure out how to free themselves of their dysfunctional programming and conditioning, to be truer to themselves.

Do you know what you *truly* desire?

Having an idea of how to go about it is very important in life, not just for your own sake, but for every one else's as well. It will help to give you courage and strength when times are tough, it will improve all of your relationships including your own, and most of all, what is life without something bigger than we are to strive towards?

I often talk about *us* in relation to the world at large, our contribution to humanity, but understand that the closer *you* as an individual get to **your own best self**, and the closer you get to your personal dreams, that impact of who you are and what you do reverberates all over the place, it helps others follow the same path, acting as a beacon that people can navigate towards while they struggle to make sense of their own reality. And it all comes down to emotional maturity, the more you know yourself, the more you have mastery over your full being, over your past and future and your current life, the more your life becomes a manifestation of you, the real you.

As your life gets better in a healthy kind of way, so does everyone else's, keep that in mind and you'll do great!

Now, before we really dig into it, I need to go through a few things first: Understand that there are many important topics discussed in the following pages, and several books could be written on each and still not exhaust all there is to know about them. But for the purpose of this book, and what the reader can get out of it, a basic understanding will suffice to get people on the right track and move them further into their personal quests to improve the quality of their lives. Which is why I have chosen to go through many different ideas instead of trying to elaborate too deeply into individual ones. And since I've studied in many different fields but remain a true master in none, it all works out great!

Just keep in mind that the elaborations are not complete, and might never be. The collective of our greatest minds and efforts throughout history are still quite short of having clear answers as to how we work on the inside, in regards to emotions, memories, feelings, past and future, and how those things get out of balance and negatively affect us as we go through our lives. So, if some of the things I write about resonate with you, and you feel you want to learn more about them, then do a proper search on Amazon (or other book stores, resources, libraries) for works written by people who have dedicated themselves to those specific subjects in their respective specialties, and read more into them. I provide some suggestions now and then to works that have been of value in my own research.

For me, I have gone through great lengths in my own healing journey to understand myself and others at the most essential level. Decades of research, poring through mounds of high quality works by professionals and experts in their fields, a lifelong meditation practice, 15 full volumes of journaling, and more self-reflection that I can put into words... And still, I don't profess to know all the answers, and I would stay away from anyone who thinks they do. Experts with multiple degrees and a lifetime of practice still have more questions than answers, at least those that are honest enough to admit it. **We are all a work in progress**, and so is our understanding of who we are beneath all the flesh and bones, behind all our needs and desires.

Though one thing comes back time and time again, as many of our most accomplished teachers and inspired leaders have concluded; that developing a deeper relationship with ourselves **is the most important thing anyone can do**, it is the basics of growing true self-love, compassion, and the only way humanity can ever progress towards a better future.

Treat this journey with all the respect it, and you, deserve.

If reading a few books to become a more caring individual, and dedicating regular time to it, seems like too much work for you, then maybe you need to wait until your perspective changes, until life teaches you the importance of loving yourself more, and how your wounds and trauma are blocking you to the things you crave for in life. But don't wait until you reach your deathbed and all those regrets come flooding back to consciousness, *better late than never* will be of little comfort, or use, to you then.

PART 1: A Journey to Emotional Maturity, a New Era to Unfold...

*"Your task is not to seek for love, but merely to seek and find all the barriers within yourself that you have built against it..." – **Rumi***

Make no mistake of it, our lives are greatly confined by the invisible forces that get created out of our fears, our conditioning, our trauma, all of our emotions that are unbalanced and mixed up with feelings we have not yet been able to understand. Those energies become obstructions, internal divisions that affect us in ways we know little about. Oftentimes people keep moving as long as they don't feel the unseen walls they are hitting up against. But understand that everyone hits those walls on a regular basis without even noticing because they have become insensitive to their emotional suffering. They have become so conditioned to accepting dead end roads that they fail to feel the signs flashing in their subconscious trying to tell them that life could be much more that what they are currently experiencing, their "emotional blindness" makes them miss out on all the most important turns that could lead them down much better roads. And it is not because you are "moving up" in your career, increasing your salary and influence and such that it means you are not blocked, hitting internal walls. People often confuse external success for overall improvements in their lives. The most important walls we hit against are those that prevent us from deeper love, true connectedness with others, and a real sense of self, who you truly are, and what you really desire out of life, the crucial elements that can make you feel like singing and dancing every single day.

That is one of the most important part of this journey, to feel the truth of who you are, to know what you are made of, and what you are truly capable of. To bring forth all of your talents and capabilities, and to blow away all of those limits that you were made to believe you couldn't overcome, or didn't even know you had. But before we get there, we must unravel, peel the layers, of the trauma and wounds we carry, all the false beliefs imposed by others and our own conditioned reasoning processes, and to ***genuinely grow in emotional maturity***.

There is pain involved in this journey, but when done right, the pain does not last long, and the results can be quite liberating. And those that are squeamish about experiencing the emotional pain that they have within themselves, understand that if you do not face it with courage directly, you will keep feeling it at a low (and sometimes not so low) level for all of your life. Like peeling off a band-aid and taking 40 years to do it, instead of doing it once, and then it's over. Yes, that one time can hurt like hell, but at least it will give the wound underneath the band-aid a chance to heal, and be treated with care. While if you peel the band-aid for 40 years, the wound will only start healing once the band-aid is off completely, and by then, the wound could be so infected that it might not even have a chance to heal before you die. That is a sad reality for many people, so don't be like those too afraid to face themselves, choose to free yourself from your emotional past now, to rid yourself from the baggage and programming that you carry, and then life will become richer and more gratifying.

The thing that drives us most in life, beyond survival needs and basic relationships, is the need to expand and express our deeper selves, to get meaning out of our lives and existence, to know what it feels like to be at our peak doing something that makes great sense to us, that is an optimum match to our greatest abilities. And the only way to do that, is to develop a good understanding of yourself, and find greater inner balance and peace with who you are and your place in this world. Not completely, not perfectly, but enough to make a difference in the best way you know how. I'm not talking about a specific destiny, but one you *evolve* as you get to know yourself better.

"We need to take out the big guns in our new revolution, that is the only way humanity can steer the ship to more fruitful shores, not in search of outer treasures as we have done in the past, but in inner ones..." – **Me**

Yep, I quote myself at times, a bit of self "back-patting" once in a while for words that stand out doesn't hurt a person to feel better about themselves...

The opening text from Krishnamurti at the beginning reflects that, each and every one of us responsible for not only how we can manage to make a superb life for ourselves, but also in "sharing a responsibility for the world", the way it is, all the good and the bad of it. That is **THE E.Q. REVOLUTION**, mastering ourselves from the inside out, and making the world change with every step each one of us takes on that journey. Not only for love, not only for happiness, but for all the incremental changes in all facets of our life. But for that to happen, we need to grow the courage to look at ourselves, and others, as we actually are.

How Healing is Associated with Increasing your Level of Emotional Maturity

To see yourself, and the world, as they are is not as easy as it might sound. Our perceptions constantly change depending on how well we are doing within ourselves, our life experiences, our unhealed wounds and conditioning, and what we are trying to get out of our lives and the people around us. If at some point in your life you have been a victim of an armed mugging from a man who pulled out a gun from his back pocket, and years later you see another man walking down the sidewalk putting his hand behind his back, you might instantly freeze, run away, or at least be very cautious, wondering if he's about to pull out a gun like that other time years back. But another person might see by the position of his hand/arm and the way it moves up and down for what he is actually doing, which is only scratching his back. Those that have no trauma related to a man with his hand behind his back can easily perceive the same position and motion that they themselves have when they scratch their own backs, so the truth of that moment is more clear to them. The emotions and feelings of the person that was mugged have been tainted, changed by the experience of being mugged, and so has their capacity to see things, and their own self, as they are. This example of the mugging, and how any past experience can modify our perceptions, applies to almost everything that we do in life, misinterpreting so much of what we see, hear, and feel. And it also applies to our life path, what we choose to do, what we avoid, the relationships that we keep and are attracted to, or the ones we let go of. And this is merely one incident, multiply that by thousands, other situations big and small, and everything from childhood, then we can start getting a clearer picture of how our past keeps us locked into unhealthy patterns and false perceptions.

SIDE NOTE: Although I focus more on the healing part and not the success/career aspect of increasing your E.Q., understand that there is a lot of talk (and validated research) nowadays in regards to how higher E.Q. is associated to career and relationship success of all kinds, so there are many other great benefits to this path that can help you in everyday life. To help relate to the many other aspects of your life that can also improve, here is a quote to support the importance of E.Q. in areas that I don't cover as much in this book, and I'll share a few more similar quotes and anecdotes even if somewhat removed from the general topics I discuss.

"In a study of skills that distinguish star performers in every field from entry-level jobs to executive positions, the single most important factor was not IQ, advanced degrees, or technical experience, it was EQ. Of the competencies required

PART 1: A Journey to Emotional Maturity, a New Era to Unfold...

for excellence in performance in the job studies, 67% were emotional competencies..." – **Daniel Goleman**

Unlike I.Q., E.Q. can be greatly improved, but it doesn't come easily. We need to develop a better understanding of how we work from the inside out, to "see" better in ways we are not familiar with. And the only way we can see, and feel, the truth about others, and ourselves, is to heal all of those things of the past, and the conditioning that comes with them, and make necessary changes in our current environment to support those changes. Further along in the book I will relate this *"seeing things as they are"* to developing our capacity to see things with better emotional "glasses", which I call **E-Glasses**. To feel the truth of things without so many filters such as fears, trauma, selfish desires, conditioning and dysfunctional programming. That is the only way to build up true Emotional Maturity, to heal, and also to love. E.M. is to relate to the world around us for the way it is, and to other people for who they are, their intent, their desires, to see through the veil of inaccurate perceptions and expressions. And not just us, but the world itself has been created by so many false perceptions and fears, another important reason for people to take this process seriously.

Every bit of trauma we have **dissociates us from our feelings**, from our emotions, it warps our sense of self, and also warps our grasp on reality.

When we focus mostly on our senses, and on the sight of our physical eyes, we dismiss everything that goes on underneath the surface. Most people stop there, to only "trust" in what they can see and touch, but doing so is dismissing the majority of the world around us. Everyone knows just how many emotions and feelings go on within us in every passing minute, all our thoughts, our hopes and desires, but it is as if we dismiss the notion that the same goes on in everyone else. When a person develops higher E.Q., they can have a much

14

better understanding of what goes on under the surface of other people. You can see the potential of a violent person in their eyes without them having to punch you first. You can see and feel when people are being deceitful, to know not to go into a business relationship with them. You can determine how selfish a person might be on a blind date in just a few minutes, to avoid a long and painful relationship. You can spot narcissists when they are trying to manipulate you, and that is all possible through having a higher emotional intelligence, and even more so when we develop into *Emotional Maturity*. And to also see all the good in people, to be able to open yourself to trust and vulnerability, well, imagine how much better your life can get.

SIDE NOTE: As I mention both **Emotional Intelligence** and **Emotional Maturity** (Though some people use *E.I.*, I use *E.Q.* for *Emotional Quotient* as it relates to I.Q., even though I call it emotional intelligence), keep in mind that this book is about building up true **Emotional Maturity** (E.M.) through healing of emotional wounds and past trauma and building up a better relationship with yourself, towards self-love and higher levels of compassion and empathy. Although at times I do refer to basic E.Q. and simple exercises to build it, for the most part Emotional Maturity is something that can only be developed with a lot of work and care for ourselves and others. Some people consider E.Q. as simply the ability to "use" and understand our emotions and the emotions of others. For me, that is more mind games than actual Emotional Intelligence, even though it is called that. If there is no love or empathy in the equation, then at best it is a lower form of E.Q., one which serves lesser purposes, but can still be helpful at times. The true value of E.M. comes out when people start using that knowledge of themselves, and their ability to manage their emotions in a healthy way, to further the goals of humanity towards having less wars and conflicts and a much better way of life for everyone. So even though I can sometimes use E.Q. and E.M. interchangeably, I usually mean the higher forms of them, unless specified otherwise.

So, in consideration of this, if your own emotional system is out of whack, then you cannot develop higher E.M., not possible. You might still be able to learn some tricks of how to use basic E.Q., but you will not be able to truly see things as they are, to overcome your own barriers, to see the true intent in other people, not even in yourself, **so your best life will always be out of reach**. And if you cannot see the truth of your interactions, then your sense of reality gets all twisted, you don't see things as they are. A chair is a chair, sure, but a romantic relationship can be all sorts of things, good and bad, and everything in between.

That makes sense, doesn't it?

Our feelings and emotions determine much more of who we are than our skills and education, but many people seem content with defining themselves mainly by their resumes and degrees, and that is sad. The value of human productivity, how much we can contribute to our employer's wealth and goals, has become the defacto way that many people gauge their sense of identity, and in doing so, they cast away a great part of themselves into the dark waters of their subconscious.

We need to reclaim those lost parts, the parts we cast out ourselves, by others, the parts that are stuck in childhood trauma and unreconciled experiences, and how that contributes to emotional imbalances and erroneous perceptions. Seeing things clearly, piercing through the lies and pain, is a non-negotiable requirement to see our own bigger picture, who we really are, and our place in this world.

As the realities of finally growing up into emotional maturity can be much more of a challenge to accept than our adult responsibilities of debts and mortgages, I have found it useful

has recently been made available on the market, new technology that enables people to not only see distant planets, but to do so without time lapse, so in real time. One telescope was damaged in transport, water, dust, it has a dirty mirror, a few cracks in the lens, and even several spider webs in the metal tube. The other telescope is in full working order, pristine. Both of them think their telescope is fine, as the telescope that got damaged was cleaned on the outside, to look new again, and there was no internal inspection as it only had a bit of dirt on the outside, and no indication of physical failures. Now, they set up a night with clear skies, they get together, and point their telescopes at the same planet, a supposedly beautiful planet as suggested in the guide. Now the woman with the pristine telescope sees the planet for what it is, similar to Earth, but brighter colors, tall trees, pinkish clouds, erupting volcanoes. She talks to her friend, to describe what she sees in broad comments. "Beautiful isn't it, amazing, what a sight!", assuming that her friend sees the same thing. Her friend sees the planet through cobwebs, cracked lens, dirty mirror, she can make out some colors, some forms, but it's mostly blurry and muted. She responds "What!? I think it's kind of drab looking, not a place I would want to visit, much less live in. What's the point of space travel if we only have places like that to live on?". Her friend is taken aback, she never realized her friend was so difficult to please, what was she expecting, a place made of gold? From then on, if they don't compare notes, if the one with the broken telescope never goes further, if they don't talk about their experience, so much can change. Their relationship will take a hit, the one with the broken telescope might lose her interest in astronomy and space travel, and even of life in general, so dejected from what she saw, her hopes in greater worlds dashed. The one with the good telescope might go on dreaming about colonies on other planets, and might register if such a program were to be made available. The one with the broken telescope will go on with that disappointment, it might seep in all kinds of other aspects in her life. This can have such an impact in both of their lives, and in their relationship, simply because of a faulty "seeing" apparatus.

We do that **all the time**, we all have issues with how we see and feel things because we are all not fully healed, none of us are. We all have some cracked lens or another, dirt and such that prevents us from seeing (and feeling) things, us and others included, for what they are. It keeps changing our views of ourselves, of others, always affecting our decisions, our relationships, creating all sorts of barriers, preventing us from seeing great opportunities, even making us afraid of change, or from pursuing better paths. Just one interaction with a bully as a kid can crack one of our lenses, contributing to an improper "sight" for the rest of our lives if we don't find a way to let go, to heal from the trauma, to fix that faulty perception and the internal barriers created from it. To heal is to "fix" our telescope, our **E-Glasses**, fine tuning our emotional system, to see things as they are, and then be able to pursue proper avenues that match our best/higher interests.

We can get a bit of an idea of this when we clean the windows of our house or apartment, then we look outside and it all seems so much clearer, nicer, and we think "wow, those windows were much dirtier than I thought, things look much better outside now". And then little by little they get dirty again, and we don't notice, and little by little we see the world outside in a more drab kind of way. But with our emotions, the result is much more powerful, and we have so much more to gain, or to lose, if we don't look after ourselves properly.

In the prior example, every speck of dust on the mirror is like one of the many wounds we carry from our past, from relationships, from trauma. Every strand of cob web like conditioning, being told that feelings don't matter, being told that men don't cry, that women should keep their place, learning racism from our parents, that white lies are okay. To then seek out a life that is based on all sorts of dysfunctional inner components and faulty programming. People that are fully convinced that life is nothing more than a bloated bank account, fame or power, do so from a dilapidated perspective. Anyone who is capable of true love and deeper, more meaningful, relationships will attest to that. **Our truest nature is based on love and compassion**, the further away people get from that, the further into selfish pursuits their lives become. And the more they follow that lesser path, it indicates that they are in need of healing and figuring out what prevents them from seeing the truth about who they are and what is truly important in life.

The future direction of humanity's evolution depends on each individual's ability to overcome their own interior suffering, and then seek out their own best selves through whichever path they would choose.

To know ourselves and to increase our ability to see things clearly requires work and dedication. What often impedes our progress has to do with the stuff we would rather not face of ourselves. But to grow the courage to look in all the dark places within, even if we don't like what we see, and even when we would rather not face the repercussions of what we might find, is necessary. **The darkness itself is most often much scarier than the truth about what lies within it**, and dealing with what we find is most often much better than dealing with all the unhealthy patterns that those uncovered things keep creating in our lives. Is blinding yourself to just how much of a drag you feel your job is better than dealing with your fear of looking for a new job, or going back to school to get to what you would prefer? Is the comfort of being in a mildly abusive relationship, even if only verbally abusive or with many incompatibility issues, better than facing the possible loneliness of being alone?

"Emotional Intelligence is a way of recognizing, understanding, and choosing how we think, feel, and act. It

shapes our interactions with others and our understanding of ourselves. It defines how and what we learn; it allows us to set priorities; it determines the majority of our daily actions. Research suggests it is responsible for as much as 80% of the "success" in our lives." – **J. Freedman**

To deeply feel when our job no longer satisfies us, and to take the steps to remedy that situation. To keep making good choices in regards to our health, to not accept when people try to dump the emotions they no longer want to carry on us, to face the losses, to face who we are and where we are at, all of it, that is the only way to a better existence... It is not easy for sure, but do you really have something more important to do than to know yourself better, to realize what is required to make your dreams come true? Many people want to believe that, that their productivity or salary is more important than their own inner well-being, more important than building that relationship with themselves, and even from seeking out love. Hopefully you have not fallen into that deadly, life depriving trap, or you are willing to do something about it if you have. Since you are reading this, then I assume that is the case, and I hope I can help you to make it happen.

The Need to Evolve Towards a New Era for Humankind

There is so much more to Emotional Maturity than the few things I have mentioned so far, which I will elaborate throughout the remainder of this book. One of the main ideas I wish to convey, is about how I believe developing true Emotional Maturity is not only the best path anyone can take in life (not of itself, but what comes of it), **but it is also the only way the world can ever change**. Without E.M., or even E.Q., people behave more or less like animals, they surrender to lustful desires, revenge, hatred, greed, violence... Murderers and rapists are the extreme forms of it, but also those that fall into addictive behaviors, drugs, that seek to dominate over others, to control and manipulate, to hoard resources, they become very selfish and egotistical, self-centered and fearful. Constantly being triggered into fight or flight mode, anxiety and despair. It is a very unhealthy way to live, it creates all sorts of physical, emotional and psychological diseases and illnesses, and our whole world suffers greatly for it. **The more people stay in states of lower emotional intelligence and maturity, the less our overall ability to reduce the chances of war, terrorism, human trafficking, poverty and illnesses**. Facing threats like the recent pandemic becomes much more complicated and life threatening, conflicts break out everywhere, consensus on the proper course of action becomes elusive, people getting triggered into survival mode does not paint a pretty picture when projected on a planetary scale.

"When we quit thinking primarily about ourselves and our own self-preservation, we undergo a truly heroic transformation of consciousness..." – **Joseph Campbell**

And that is what it is like to live with low E.Q., constantly going into survival mode, ruled by fears and unhealthy emotions, selfish, individualistic, the whole world can burn at your feet, as long as your own house remains standing. That is why I believe the future of humanity lies within our efforts to increase our level of E.Q., towards E.M., but it needs to be on a grand scale, planet-wide... **Every person that decides to step on this path brings us a little closer to a better tomorrow, a new era for us all.** I don't believe there is any other way to see a world without wars when so many people can't even prevent themselves from falling into their internal fears. When they are divided within themselves to such a degree, that they can barely manage to control their desires and feelings, when the slightest wind sends them into fits of greed and violence, to empty the shelves of their local supermarkets, to pillage, and to see everyone around them as enemies to destroy, or competitors to conquer. There is no bright future possible for us as long as the cards are stacked against us, against our higher goals and aspirations.

"I think in the coming decade we will see well-conducted research demonstrating that emotional skills and competencies predict positive outcomes at home with one's family, in school, and at work. The real challenge is to show that emotional intelligence matters over-and-above psychological constructs that have been measured for decades like personality and IQ. I believe that emotional intelligence holds this promise..." – **Peter Salovey**

But now, put the idea of a brighter future for humanity aside for a while, this new era that could be in our grasp, and focus back on you, your own self, your best life, to make your own personal dreams come true, that is the best part in all of this. Make *your* life great, and you don't even need to worry your pretty little self about the big picture, it will all work out in the end. As long as you work on your own healing journey, to make your life awesome and loving, then everything you do will end up serving the whole in the same beneficial way, I'll make that point clear.

Keep in mind that perfect solutions do not exist, and even though we might be responsible for making the world the way it is, we don't need to stress over it. As long as the foundation of whatever we choose to do is based on love and compassion, then whatever we build will also be based on those higher values. Does this make sense to you, does this look like it can make this world of ours a great place to live in? Those are the choices that we face, and the decisions that we need to make. Again, there is no perfect solution, if it makes sense to you, then why not? Who decides what is right and what is wrong, who do you allow to judge your own feelings, and why can't love actually *be* the answer? Not love for love's sake, not in marriage and 'till death do us part, but in what we do from a

PART 1: A Journey to Emotional Maturity, a New Era to Unfold...

more loving sense of self, our actions that create the world we live in, not in how we confine ourselves, how we live within the four walls we call home, but of our impact on a global scale.

Those are the rewards that await the ones who dare to do what is required to build up *Emotional Maturity*, the greater good for everyone starts with the greater good for *you*, a healthy balance between personal desires and what you create in our world. And as it all starts with you, that brings me to something very important, so important it should never be forgotten.

Be Kind to Yourself, isn't it all about Love Anyway?

You probably have guessed by now why I mentioned in the introduction that this book isn't your average E.Q. building guide, the type that promises to get you a job offer or prepare you for your next blind date, it is much more involved than that. I believe that to truly increase our E.Q., to get the most long lasting benefits from it, requires an all encompassing method. Not that there is any one particular method, but at the very least we must consider most aspects of our lives, from way back in our past, to everything that makes up our daily existence. And yes, that requires work, and lots of love for ourselves and others. So, remember to be kind to yourself along the way. The road *will* get bumpy at times, the only way we can grow is to know how to get through those bumps in the best way possible.

"Searching all directions with one's awareness, one finds no one dearer than oneself. In the same way, others are dear to themselves. So one should not hurt others if one loves oneself..." – **From the Udāna, Pali Canon**

<u>Which basically means</u>: You are the one most deserving of your love, and the more you love yourself, the less you should hurt others, so, the more you will love them as well, as they are also deserving of love, yours, and their own. That is the cycle of love that can make this place of ours into whatever we dream of it.

To Love Yourself Completely

Being kind to yourself, *all* of you, your past, your current situation, decisions, experiences, is one of the most important things you can do. Otherwise what you are saying is that parts of you are not important in your life, so might as well cast them out into the deep dark depths of your subconscious and forget they are even there. By the way, that is what we do with our trauma, experiences we keep regretting, shameful of, parts of us that have experienced painful things in the past, that are hurt and suffering, left in our subconscious to rot like forgotten prisoners in abandoned castles of old, in *oubliettes*. It might not be so fun to think of it that way, but that's pretty much how it is. Being kind to ourselves is to accept our faults, accept our history, and yes, even to accept everything that has happened to us and everything we have done. Because no matter how bad and ugly things might have gotten, if we try to forget those experiences and feelings, to not accept them as our "real" past and not just some kind of nightmare to forget, then those parts of us that have suffered will always be kept in that suffering until we finally accept all of it, and do whatever we can to let go and reclaim those parts into our present lives.

Those parts are not shameful for their experiences, for what people have done to them (or you to others), they are not ugly, and they don't deserve to remain in obscure parts of your being. This has a lot to do with our healing journey.

So again, first and foremost, be kind to yourself, **ALL** of yourself. That is the basic foundation of building self-love, and self-love is the basic foundation required to truly heal ourselves and live a life that is meaningful and up to whatever dream we might make of it. Self-love is the most basic starting point for whatever your beliefs are in life, true unconditional love, souls, God, Universal Consciousness, Heaven, Buddhism, anything, even if your beliefs end on the surface of your skin, it all starts with self-love, always, including building up E.M.. Obviously, if you are a sociopath who is only interested in world domination, then self-love is nothing more than an obstacle in your way, as with compassion and empathy. For a sociopath, self-love might make them hesitate a while before dumping toxic chemicals in someone else's backyard, or they might reconsider using slave labor from poor countries to manufacture their products, which would mean lower profit margins and longer expansion periods. For them, self-love is something to stay clear of, but for everyone else that hasn't completely lost their connection to their soul, or their inner-self, or even the desire to build healthy reciprocal relationships with people, then the strongest foundation begins with self-love, always.

SIDE NOTE: Sometimes I use "God", and soul, or other similar descriptors and terms. I know that we all have our own beliefs, and I generally keep to non-belief systems, but most people that are interested in healing believe in at least *something* beyond what their eyes can see, other realities, God, the intelligence of the Universe... So if you don't believe in God per se, substitute for what you *do* believe in. If you believe in nothing beyond what you can touch, then you can still get something in regards to healing and increasing your level of E.Q., the choice is yours. If you take offense on hearing/reading the word "God" or "Soul", then take this time to understand where those feelings come from, and why you are feeling that way, another emotional growth opportunity, you lucky person you!

If Life were so Easy

Evidently, it isn't so simple as to just say "I love myself" while brushing your teeth in the morning, and go on with your daily routine and expect to achieve true meaning deep within, or any appreciable increase in E.M..

We are all complicated creatures, we all struggle on a regular basis with a mix of emotions and feelings we don't quite understand, needs and desires we struggle to satisfy, it is part of being human. Yes, I have mentioned that we are all wounded, we all have trauma from our past that is unhealed, dysfunctional programming... But those inner dysfunctions, those things that need our love, they don't make us "defective" or unlovable. As children, we often associate not being perfect as the same as not being lovable, something we carry well into our adult lives. It is easy to associate doing something bad with receiving less hugs as children, then believing it makes us less lovable in the process, and with repeated experiences like that, unhealthy patterns emerge. Not thinking we are lovable might be one of the major "dysfunctional programming" we need to let go of.

"The most beautiful people we have known are those who have known defeat, known suffering, known struggle, known loss, and have found their way out of the depths. These persons have an appreciation, a sensitivity and an understanding of life that fills them with compassion, gentleness, and a deep loving concern. Beautiful people do not just happen..." – **Elisabeth Kübler-Ross**

As we go further down this road, when we start identifying the sources of present day pain, the conflicts we deal with, the parts of our lives that are less perfect, and then make decisions to remove those points of suffering from our lives... At some point it might appear that we judge others, and ourselves. But doing what is best for you doesn't automatically translate to judging others for who they are. If a person is physically abusing you, present or past, and you decide that your love for yourself is worth pulling out from that relationship, you don't need to see that person as evil to make the call. The other person might feel that way, but that is on them, not you, and yes, that happens. People will feel judged, they might feel "unlovable" when you decide to take a step back to figure things out, or to completely remove yourself from those relationships, but again, *you* are worth it. And that goes the same for any part of you that you feel might be inadequate, imperfect, to not judge, or cast out those parts that you have a hard time accepting, but to build a relationship with them. With others, you can do the same with a few people that you feel are more in line with where you need to go, but of course with yourself, you need to do it fully, you can't be choosy with what you accept, and what you don't. That is why building up self-love can be tricky, but very necessary.

QUICK TIP: The importance of breathing. Building up emotional maturity, all the work involved, can take a toll on our level of energy, physical and emotional. You can expect to need more sleep during the periods you are most active in your efforts, more down-time, vacations, ways to soothe yourself. It is a whole body experience that requires the presence and connection to your whole body, and healthy breathing is a big part of it. And to consider that the less presence you are capable of, the more the most important aspects of life pass you by. This exercise doesn't require much effort, just to be mindful of your breath as it goes in and out of your lungs. You can imagine the air as charged particles that bring life sustaining oxygen to your entire system, your whole body, which nourishes you with every breath you take in, and expels contaminants with every exhaled breath. You can do this anywhere, and anytime you feel tense, disconnected, and just a minute or two of mindful breathing is often enough to reset your energies.

Again, to build self-love, it not only requires us to peer deep into our past and see things as what they are, and were, but also to look deeply in our present as well, to identify people, environments and situations, and our own behavior, that does not support a higher love for ourselves. Difficult decisions will need to be taken, seeing things from a *better/different* light is also necessary, **otherwise how can you see what you were not able to see before?** It is one thing to see with our physical eyes, but quite another to see the world through the eyes of our heart.

What is the difference?

Seeing with our eyes, we tend to focus on the physical world, and we also tend to be selfish and locked within our own mind, our ego. Only the practical/survival aspects of existence populate our thoughts and feelings, purpose and meaning continuously elude us. But, seeing the world through the "eyes" of your heart (more on that later), you see through love, through compassion, you feel and experience your emotions and feelings as they are, beyond all the filters and conditioning of your mind, like fear, jealousy, greed, trauma... If everyone could experience life through their healed hearts, Earth would be like Heaven, or a tropical paradise, but that would require a massive amount of self-love throughout the whole planet, sustained and shared to heal every wound that every person carries. We are surely not there, maybe humanity is unable to love to that extent, but we are definitely in need of more of it.

While I'm at it, on self-love and overcoming dysfunctional programming, I will do a bit of it myself right now: *"This work is not perfect, I am not perfect, you are not perfect, no one is perfect..."*. Let us all keep that in mind and you, and I, will blow the roof off this place!

So, be kind to yourself throughout this whole journey, as if you are trying to "woo" yourself, like a person aching to make the best impression while going on a first date. Again, after all, aren't you worth it?

Unconditional Love?

Talking about self-love made me consider how people's ideas of love can be so different from one person to the next, assorted notions and expectations, and many might even consider self-love as something selfish, but it is far from it. Now, not to say that my understandings of love are so great, so "perfect", but people must arm themselves with as much information on love as they can.

Now, I'm talking about actual love, not the romantic love that most people consider as love, but real love, true **unconditional** love. The kind that comes from deep within you, or I should say *enters* from deep within you, not from books, not from simple techniques, nor from Hollywood movies. I am talking about true love, the kind of love that shines from your eyes like laser beams, or at times a soft compassionate glow, and can't be mistaken for anything else. It is beyond gestures or words, true love is a very deep feeling of gratitude and compassion, to see the needs of everyone just as important as your own, yet knowing it must start within yourself first.

As love for you, all of you, is the main tool to properly process trauma, to overcome the negative impact of wounds and past experience, and also to make healthy decisions in regards to your current habits and life path, it is important to understand what it is, and what it isn't, at least to a certain workable degree.

"I found in my research that the biggest reason people aren't more self-compassionate is that they are afraid they'll become self-indulgent. They believe self-criticism is what keeps them in line. Most people have gotten it wrong because our culture says being hard on yourself is the way to be..."
– Dr. Kristin Neff

On Unconditional Love: I wish people would take the time to understand themselves better, instead of repeatedly throwing themselves head first into romantic notions then experience devastating heartbreaks because they fell for wrongful ideas and ill conceived attempts at "making" someone love them, or for what they "thought" love was. Then the false love that was built between them eventually crumbles into dust, because it

31

was never love to begin with. And if people would spend more time understanding themselves, healing, then they would not seek out the "love" of others with such indulgence and desperation.

I get it, we all crave love and affection, but please, **for the love of yourself**, take the time to know what love actually is, and what it isn't. That doesn't mean to avoid romantic relationships, but don't "give out" your soul thinking that you are offering your love as a fair exchange. Your soul is yours to keep, love is *shared*, not offered on a pedestal for anyone to consume. If the person you choose to be with has a limited capacity to share love, then accept that, or move on. We are *all* limited in our ability to truly love, no exception. Relationships are much more about sharing of ourselves than "falling in love". We develop bonds, we share resources, we have sex, make and raise children, and *share* the love we develop within ourselves, nothing to give.

The idea of "self-love" is not in the pampering, me first selfish kind of way. But by being a conduit to love itself, true unconditional love... Loving others as much as ourselves, to have the capacity to love 7.5 billion people, or at least, to consider their overall needs in a way that matches your capacities. That is why this path is the most unselfish, as long as we understand what real love is.

HARDLININGIT: First, unconditional love IS NOT about giving YOURSELF away to someone without asking or expecting anything in return, to do everything, to buy everything, to drain your soul into another person without worry or care of what you "might" get back. That is BLIND DEVOTION, not unconditional love. For true unconditional love, first, YOU must also be part of the equation *in equal measure*, you cannot dismiss your own love for yourself in the process. The person's intent in receiving what you give them must also be part of the equation. If the person receives in a selfish manner, that is not unconditional love. For there to be real love, ALL parts of the experience and exchange must be in compassion and care. People that profess of being hurt by "unconditional love" are unfortunately quite nescient of what love really is.

SIDE NOTE: And no, I don't use caps so frequently, but this is quite an important topic, and one where many people lose themselves in relationships without knowing why, or if alone, continually ache for something that no one can ever give them anyway, as true love can only come from within them, so I indulged a bit, for effect...

"Love is a flame that burns everything other than itself. It is the destruction of all that is false and the fulfillment of all that is true..." – **Adyashanti**

And I am making a special note of this for a few reasons: To know that what people believe in is very important in regards to what becomes of our reality, what becomes of our future, for all of us. When there is a mass influence of misinformation, erroneous perceptions, it can be very detrimental to how things come to be on our planet. It becomes a sort of mass hypnosis that pulls us further away from the truth, and further away from our true selves. It works against us from the inside out, and creates a mess in the process. And love is one of the main things that we *need* to get right. And the longer we continue with those "un-truths", not only do we cause more harm, but there is much more damage to undo further down the line. Think of times when people of color had very few rights, even to step onto a bus, or go eat in a restaurant, and for the people living in those times, this was **"how things were"**, until some decided to challenge it at great cost to them. Or even the power we have given some words, one in particular, to become so hurtful that many people even today would be seen as very mean/racist to even use it, me included. Yet, we are the ones who have given our power to those words and situations, and we are the ones who can take that power back, we are in control, it is our decision. When women were not allowed to vote, and people thought it was just common sense in those days, that ignorance became their truth, until people fought against this "un-truth" that some had created. We decide our future in many unseen ways, we decide what our fate shall become, and to do that, we need to seek out the truth in all its shapes and forms, and to stop giving our power to things that should not be.

When we give our power to words and ideas that result in destructive forces, we *all lose* as those destructive forces that derive power from ourselves hang over our heads like swords of Damocles.

So again, those that say they gave "all" for the sake of "unconditional love", but got burnt... No, love never burns anyone, not true love. When we truly share in unconditional love, there is never any pain (well, maybe from the losses of what wasn't love), no regret, and no burns or callouses... When we give conditionally, then, yes, but it is because even if we "say" we don't expect anything in return, we actually do, otherwise you would never look back at what you gave versus what you received. If people took just a bit of time to truly consider what *unconditional* means, it would make sense that it *cannot* result in any pain, or drain, whatsoever. Growing up in emotional maturity is also about knowing what we can expect from others, and what we shouldn't, that lessens the burden on relationships, and brings us more peace of mind, whether in a romantic relationship, or not.

A lot of people ache for a kind of love that just does not exist, and that ache affects everyone.

Now, don't get me wrong, romantic love is cool too, I'm not advocating to forsake it altogether, but romantic love comes and goes, while unconditional love is a very different thing, words to the wise, that's all I'm saying...

"Freedom and love go together. Love is not a reaction. If I love you because you love me, that is mere trade, a thing to be bought in the market; it is not love. To love is not to ask anything in return, not even to feel that you are giving something- and it is only such love that can know freedom..."
– Jiddu Krishnamurti

I think for the most part everyone knows this to a certain extent, but sometimes our romantic hopes can get the best of us, and might be working in the background mostly unnoticed. So to assert these realities out loud can help us to filter out what is real, and what isn't.

How True Love Manifests in People

Another way of considering love, as it is an important aspect for everything that we do in life and the basis to striving towards a better humanity in general, is this:

Love is not a single thing, and not so easy to define even though we all try to, so it is worth getting into it a bit more before I move on to other sections. I mean, for thousands of years writers, poets, philosophers, and even scientists have been trying to explain it, express it, and even box it into pretty little categories and quaint gift cards. We don't quite have a tight grip on what it actually is, and I guess that's the point of it, it refuses to be held back for any reason, for any "condition". Some people would say going through the effort to plan, and the cost, of a fancy meal at a restaurant is love, yet narcissists can do that very well, and they are known to not have the capacity to feel much of anything, including love, so then what is the difference? Others would say that making sandwiches for homeless people is love, which could be, but then not necessarily, as some might only do it as a highlight on their resume for increased employability, as in "I care, look at how I have spent some of my free time!".

So how can people know if they are truly loving individuals, or not so much?

The frequency that you do "loving" things, your heartfelt intent while you are doing them, how you regularly treat yourself, and others, and how you spend most of your time will give you an idea. But love is mostly a personal thing, even if you can spot it at times in others, it can be hard to know for sure. So it is best to work towards love gradually, and not worry about "how much" you think you can love, or not.

Keep in mind that the more you heal your trauma, overcome your wounds, forgive, let go, the more **love will automatically grace your life**, no questions asked, no thinking required. Like the previous quote, about love coming to those that remove the barriers to it, you will feel it more often, and at a deeper level, experiencing less negative thoughts, less unhealthy emotions. Although I spoke of different kinds of love, in this book I will generally refer to love as true love, as "unconditional" as possible, and not romantic or familiar.

> *"When you adopt the viewpoint that there is nothing that exists that is not part of you, that there is no one who exists who is not part of you, that any judgment you make is self-judgment, that any criticism you level is self-criticism, you will wisely extend to yourself an unconditional love that will be the light of the world..."* – **Harry Palmer**

The more we heal, the more we develop love for ourselves, the more that love becomes unconditional. As all of our wounds, our trauma, our fears and judgments, all create a wide array of conditions, and those conditions taint the world around us in all sorts of distorted shapes and colors, and they all decrease our ability to love unconditionally. And that is one good benefit of increasing our Emotional Maturity, to start seeing ourselves as we truly are, **instead of who we want to believe we are**.

If people would suddenly gain the ability to see and feel just how little they can actually, truly love, then everyone would face the truth about their actions, about how selfish they/we truly are. It would be devastating for most people. If something like that would happen, it would be a great opportunity of change for all of humanity, but there would be a transitional process that would be harsh and severally depressing. At least we would know that we are all in this together, that we are all not even remotely close to as loving as we think of ourselves as, and if we had the true courage to face it, then there would be much more hope for the future of us all.

Again, this might sound a bit deflating, but to truly love, to become Emotionally Mature, we cannot remain in the darkness of our ignorance, and people's lack of self-love is one of those things that most people are reluctant to face, *but we must* in order to grow and live a life much closer to that which we dream of.

I suggest to everyone to find some good books and resources on what truly loving yourself means. For now, consider these typical behaviors for yourself, and those around you, to give you an idea of the habits you might need to change, and of your progress. No one is perfect, everyone can exhibit very loving traits at times, and very unloving traits at other times. But generally people tend towards one or the other, again, it's all in the balance.

Generally, loving people do these things:

- They don't call themselves bad words (stupid, ignorant, lazy)
- They don't accept negative thinking (I'll never make it on time, I'm not good enough for that, I'll never find someone to love me)
- They don't hang around toxic people (more on that later)
- They sustain healthy habits (eating, exercise, yoga, meditation)
- They don't do stuff to cause harm to their bodies (excessive alcohol consumption, drugs, extreme/dangerous sports, over-eating)
- They make good/healthy decisions for themselves and those around them
- They regularly consider other people's needs, but not in self-serving ways, and not at their greater detriment
- They consider the emotional impact they have on others
- They have the ability to feel what it's like to be in another person's situation (this is more rare/difficult than most people think)
- They have true compassion and empathy for others

Again, no one is perfect, and many people "appear" okay in normal situations, seem loving enough, so it might be better to consider them, and yourself, more carefully in times of conflict and turmoil, when you're not *trying* to be at your best for anyone. That is the true measure of a person, of their hearts, what they do when they think no one is around to see anything, or when they can't stifle their reactions.

To get back to the beginning of this section, not only is self-love not selfish as some might make you believe, it is actually the most unselfish thing anyone can do, not just for themselves, but for others. As the more truly loving we become, we just can't help ourselves from sharing that love, and devoting our lives to helping others. I wish my awareness and writing skills were more developed on this important subject, to maybe go well beyond our current understanding and knowledge, but this will need to suffice for now.

From Emotional Intelligence to Emotional Maturity, and Everything in Between

"When we accept and embrace our emotions as the way they are rather than what we wish them to be and discover that in the deepest darkest moments, we are okay – this is the true emotional healing. Emotional healing is when you face your worst fears only to realize you are okay. You have no control over what life throws at you, but you have control of how to relate to whatever comes your way..." — **Susan Wenzel**

What kind of World do *you* want to Live in?

Think about this: Animals seek to survive at all costs, they don't think of right or wrong, they don't think of the future or the past, they don't consider the greater impact their existence has on others, or on the future of their species. They generally live day by day, and follow the rules of the herd, or live solitary existences. What truly separates humans from animals, *is our ability to consider the welfare of our species on a grand scale*, to show love and compassion even to those who have nothing to bring us, to have developed extensive ways of caring for our wounded and sick, and to be able to consider our own well being in very intricate manners. People with low E.M. and anti-social behaviors **often work *against* the healthy survival of our species**, they hoard resources, they easily get angry and violent, abusive, jealous, greedy, seek revenge, they become murderers and rapists, they cheat and steal, and cause all sorts of harm in our societies. They get triggered in survival mode on a regular basis, which pulls them away from love and empathy, from higher values and morals, and instead fall into their own animal nature, back to operating from the primitive lizard brain and associated chemical responses.

From Emotional Intelligence to Emotional Maturity, and Everything in Between

Our world suffers greatly from people who remain in low E.M. mode. Narcissists (and others in the "Dark Triad"), even though they might be able to learn and mimic some E.Q. tricks and manipulate people with them, are not considered high in E.Q. in my opinion, not in the emotionally mature kind of way.

The greatest advantage humans have lies not in our ability to create technology, to build massive cities or go to the moon, but to develop a better relationship with all of our selves, to go beyond our animal heritage and primitive ancestry, to move out of the caves of our past, and become truly loving beings. Everything that is associated with developing higher emotional maturity gets compounded many times over when considering the long term benefits, such as reduced; wars, murders, drug use, human trafficking, violence and abuse of our children, spousal abuse, terrorism, and the list goes on, and on. That following this path could be a decision that requires thought is beyond me, **we should all just embrace it and hang on tight!**

To clean up the environment so that our children inherit a "clean" Earth might not be the least of our worries, but as long as we don't grow in our own maturity, *there will always be litter bugs to make new messes to clean up tomorrow.* Problems will never go away as long as we don't change the things inside of us that create the problems in the first place. I don't know about you, but I do believe we can do much more than our current model of society, the work routines that leave people drained, the often ill suited education structure and content, people struggling to find a bit of time to relax or to develop greater relationships, all the violence and pollution, criminal rates, growing terrorism... What we are doing right now ain't working very well, and there's no clear indication that things will get better no matter how much time passes.

So again, what kind of world do you really want to live in?

PART 1: A Journey to Emotional Maturity, a New Era to Unfold...

Are you okay with the amount of terrorism, the constant threat of war, the idea of millions of humans being trafficked every year, growing depression and suicide rates, the expanding use of drugs to get our children compliant to our schedules and societal needs... Even if for your own sake, developing emotional maturity is well worth the effort, the improvements of those other aspects of life comes with the package deal, no sticker shock as with extras on a new car. And who knows what else will start growing inside of you once you start feeding yourself higher quality nutrients.

When I think back of my own efforts of participation in the grand scheme of things, I have had a tendency to get caught up in all the work that "appeared" to require attention, and the frustrations of seeing things cycle all over again back to where they all began. Time and time again I have noticed that as long as people, and I, don't change inside, we are just smearing problems around, a little less here, and a bit more over there. We have a very limited capacity to create true, lasting change as long as the change doesn't start deep within us. That is why I felt the only solution that made sense to me, after I realized it and spent the many years required to do the work to start making it happen for myself (and still working on it), was to convince others of that truth, and to help them do something about it. I'll say it again, it is not easy for sure, but if you really do believe that we can strive towards a brighter future instead of merely surviving like our primitive ancestors, then find a way to **summon up some courage and strength and carry forth to make it all come true!**

With Emotional Maturity, your courage will grow as your path calls for it, as long as you are following a good one, words of encouragement.

MUSICAL INTERLUDE: Try this one: *Take me Home,* by **Jess Glynne** (The official video with only her is a pretty good one)

Remember that we are responsible for allowing the world to remain as it is, the decision makers can only suggest, or attempt to force us to comply, but in the end, *we decide,* and we also decide how far we want to go to make anything happen, and again, it starts within each and everyone of us:)

Emotional Intelligence versus Emotional Maturity

I will take a bit of extra time here to elaborate more on what I mean by emotional maturity, since there has been a fair amount of talk about *emotional intelligence* these past few years, and it is after all the main topic of this book.

Unfortunately many would try to make us believe that emotional intelligence is something that can be easily learnt with a few tips and techniques, and that's the end of it. The true power of mastering through our emotions is not merely to learn a few "tricks of the trade", narcissists and sociopaths can do that for the sole purpose of controlling and manipulating others, which makes our whole society the worst for the knowledge when applied for the wrong reasons, and also part of why I feel it is important to get it right before we go too far ahead with it. Manipulative CEO's and other decision makers can learn all sorts of techniques to coerce and subvert their employees into productivity through E.Q., but those that do are not great leaders, they are simply abusers of trust and authority, so the repercussions can have such a vast impact in so many aspects of our lives when the people in charge are not using it with good intents.

PART 1: A Journey to Emotional Maturity, a New Era to Unfold...

Yes, simple techniques can be learned to control our emotions that can give us the *appearance* of developing higher Emotional Intelligence, but emotions are not simply things to toy around with and to control. We can learn techniques to read faster, to be more adept at calculating in our minds, or learning a language faster, but emotions are integral to **who we are as humans**, they are part of our self-expression, of our actual self, not something to simply categorize and discard. In a way, high E.Q./E.M. can be like a small "super power" over people that don't have much of it, so some take advantage. But as I mentioned, for me Emotional Maturity involves love and compassion alongside emotional intelligence, it is to use that knowledge for good, for yourself and others included.

A person that has taken the time to heal their trauma and wounds, to truly know themselves deep within, to develop love and compassion, to make painful choices in their current environment to support their path, cannot take advantage of what they have learned along the way, that is the "mature" part, to use that "super power" in a loving and responsible way. That is why narcissistic and Dark Triad types (which I will better define in a further section) can never develop emotional maturity, they would need to heal whatever pain is within them that makes them narcissistic and sociopathic, to not be that any longer before they can make any progress on the road to emotional maturity.

"As human beings we all want to be happy and free from misery... we have learned that the key to happiness is inner peace. The greatest obstacles to inner peace are disturbing emotions such as anger, attachment, fear and suspicion, while love and compassion and a sense of universal responsibility are the sources of peace and happiness..."
– Dalai Lama

From Emotional Intelligence to Emotional Maturity, and Everything in Between

The darkest clouds can create the most beautiful rainbows, but only after they have let go of the weight they were carrying. That is what separates the weak from the strong, those that have the courage to face their worst fears, their deepest desires, all of their flaws and shortcomings, and of what is required to uncover their best gifts as well.

But a lot of people still consider E.Q. as *any* form of control or understanding of emotions, so I needed to take it into consideration in my explanations. And maybe it is in a certain way, a diabolical genius can still be a genius, so narcissists and sociopaths might be somewhat intelligent in E.Q., but I wouldn't write home about it if I were them. If they did write home about it, it might go something like: "*I am totally devoid of any capacity to love, and I don't care a smidgen about anyone else but me, but luckily I am gifted in the knowledge of emotions with which I can manipulate and control people, and can even make my partner believe I actually love him/her. And with my ease in domination tactics, I have increased profit margins of my business by 30%. So what if heart attacks from my employees have sharply risen, burn-outs a daily occurrence, suicides have tripled, at least the shareholders are happy, what else is more important? Well, that and my own terrific, splendid image!*".

Aaaaannnd wait for it, now!: Cue in the evil laugh, just before the letter would burst into flames, obviously, where do you think the "home" that they write to is at? Ha, I'm kidding, no I'm not, well a little, not really... Hmm, seems like I've got some inner discrepancies to work on... I had to get into this, sooner rather than later, as to develop in emotional maturity, we need to understand the greatest impediments to our efforts, not only to identify them within us, but in others as well. Being around people like that can seem "adventurous" and entertaining, and they can even seem like role models we want to follow for everything they get done, as long as we don't scratch the thin veneer of their inflated ego and almost god like abilities to transform smoke and mirrors into fantastical lifelike creations of materialism. Yet somehow they always leave us dreadfully drained in the end, almost dead, as if our soul had been sucked out through every orifice we had left unprotected and open to them, go figure.

Which somehow leads me to trauma, another very important aspect we need to tackle on our path to emancipation.

(Yeah, I use acanthous humor at times, to break up the often serious tone. We are all human and imperfect, and too much seriousness can make our brains switch off now and then. And besides, even though the topic is important and indeed serious, it is best not to take ourselves *too* seriously, otherwise we might distance ourselves from our self-love, which is even more essential than whatever manner of delivery I might choose to convey the message, well, mostly.)

On Trauma

This might seem like a big leap, from unconditional love to trauma, with narcissism layered somewhere in between, but think about it, it kind of makes sense. Like both ends of a fractured ring, right there, so close together, yet there is a gap, and the only real way of going from one end to the other, is the long way around, to get to "almost" the same place. Yet most people get stuck looking across the gap, aching for a different shore, avoiding to look at the things behind them, not wanting to journey that long road for something that is right in front of them, yet will remain forever out of their reach. Trauma, and all associated dysfunctions and unhealthy conditioning, is what keeps us from love, they are the barriers we need to remove from our system to not only build healthy E.M., but to love and be happy in a lasting kind of way. When we grow up the courage to turn back, to face all of those things of the past, all our shortcomings, our pain, to journey back home, to our starting point, then we realize that "gap" was just an illusion, our "ring" is actually complete, but still we must go through this process to not only realize it, but to embody that truth fully. As if that gap was the echo of all the fears we did not face, and once faced and overcome, we see, and feel, us as complete.

So, the more a person works on healing from their trauma and all associated dysfunctions, the more loving they get, simple as that, as the more we can bridge that gap, the more that love can flow through us.

But what is "trauma" exactly?

Not that there is "one" exact definition, but many people have misconceptions about what it is. Many people think you can only get "trauma" by being heavily abused in childhood, either physically of sexually, or from wars and such. But trauma is much more widespread than that. We **ALL** have emotional and psychological trauma, it is a part of being human. We cannot live through our lives and escape it. If we were without trauma whatsoever, we would all be saints and gurus, actually, the highest forms of them, "God-like" in a way. Trauma can be seen as imperfections in our energy systems, our emotions, our body, anything that prevents our being from functioning to its fullest capacity. Without it, we would be "perfect", which I don't think is actually possible to be perfect in human form. Some belief systems consider that once a person achieves such a state of perfection, they just dissipate into nothingness, as the physical world cannot contain such a perfect being. Not that I believe exactly that, but still, something along the lines of us not having the capacity to be perfect.

"Healing is like an onion. As you process through one layer of trauma to release the pain and heal, a new layer will surface. One layer after another layer will bring up new issues to focus on. Pace yourself. Only focus on one layer at a time..."
– Dana Arcuri

So, consider trauma as anything that stands in between the everyday you, meaning the one that does what he/she can to make ends meet, the one that acts in selfish ways more than they would care to be aware of, the one that keeps tripping up on all sorts of little issues and acts mainly from the ego. So, all the pain, all the dysfunctions, all the conditioning, that is what I consider as trauma, all falling under that "trauma" umbrella. And then there is the "un-traumatized" you, the one that is truly loving and compassionate, the one that is the hero, or heroine, the one that aches for a better life, the one that dreams and the one that wishes they would get to know love on a more intimate, up close, level. The fully realized being that is capable of doing whatever they set their mind to, the "almost" perfect friend/lover/parent, who knows what to say and when to say it, that has mastered their inner world and all that jazz... You can even think of your "un-traumatized" self as your soul, and trauma is the stuff that prevents your soul from fully merging with your body, to express itself fully through it.

So, everything that is between those two versions of you, I call trauma, which might not be the absolute best definition of it, but to not over-complicate things, let's say we can call all that stuff trauma. **Heal and reconcile your trauma, and the gap between those two versions of you diminishes**, you become more loving and compassionate, and your life begins to reflect that new reality, from that new "more whole/less fractured" you. That is my definition of trauma that I use in this book, as an attempt to simplify things and keep it consistent.

From Emotional Intelligence to Emotional Maturity, and Everything in Between

The more trauma we have, the more our body feels bruised and battered, and our awareness just remains in the mind, in the ego, as the body becomes too scary to move into, and we end up neglecting our emotions, our feelings, disconnected more and more, and life becomes more of an illusion to us, and then we feel disconnected from others as well. Then everyone become like enemies to us, people we can't trust. Trauma can be wounds from the past, conditioning, judgments, hatred, grudges, envy, regrets, shame, racism, needs to control, anything within you that causes disruptions in your system, creates and sustains dysfunctional programming, that warps your sense of self, that cause unhealthy emotional reactions and feelings, that pulls you away from love and compassion... Not that greed and those other "negative" emotions and feelings within themselves are trauma, but they get created out of it. So again, I use trauma as a bit of a "catch all" term to mean anything that separates the "external" you, from the deeper "internal" you, the one that is connected to the deepest love possible.

I will not go too deeply into trauma here, as I expand upon it in different sections, but it is important to get a basic understanding of it before reading on. Why am I making a big deal out of this you may ask? So much of the decisions we make on a regular basis are determined by our trauma, all that stuff, and all the baggage that comes along for the hellish ride. And again, since "all of that stuff" is also the greatest barriers to love, it is also the greatest barriers to a world that can exceed our expectations.

Oh, here's another way you might be able to relate to it: Consider trauma and other types of dysfunctional conditioning and their effects on you, as viruses in your system, **the more viruses you have, the less "human" your life becomes**. Like greed, jealousy, the unhealed abuses and painful experiences in your childhood, those nasty words people have told you, the yelling, the bullying, the mean boss, the loveless spouse... All those little, and sometimes big, emotional and psychological bruises, or "infections", accumulating in your being, having a similar effect as viruses. Each affecting you in their own way, making you afraid when you shouldn't be, or not afraid when you should, to make you angry, to react in mean ways, selfish, violent, greedy. Any kind of action or reaction that is unloving in nature comes from those "viruses", as if they hijack parts of you and make you succumb to their control, which is often to keep you in misery, like parasites that are aware and unwilling to lose their host. They seek their own life, and don't really care about yours, as long as you remain alive, as long as you are merely surviving and kept in misery, not thriving, that is their only requirement of you. And often that is the case, the more a person is "infected" with a host of those emotional viruses, they seek their own survival above anything else, love, empathy, companionship, deeper connectedness, all become irrelevant to them. To grow in emotional maturity is to heal your body of the various viruses that have infected it, which might make more sense than to call it trauma for some. People can gain knowledge of E.Q. while still being heavily infected by viruses, so they end up using that knowledge for very selfish, evil purposes. Hmm, starting to sound a bit like a Zombie apocalypse.

So, in that sense, **developing Emotional Maturity is a bit like building up your own Emotional Immune System**, to fight off those nasty little greed "viruses" that might make you steal from the petty cash at work or someone else's lunch, those jealousy viruses that might make you put laxatives in the coffee of the person next up for promotion, or the anger viruses that make you blow up in traffic just because someone cut in front of you, or the untrustful virus that prevents you from opening up in relationships. To see all of those "negative" emotions, and the stuff in you that causes them, as viruses to heal and remove from your system, well, that can help, I hope. And this is not to dismiss what caused those pains in the first place (like why a person might be untrustful), just an understanding of how they affect you once they are there.

And another reason why it makes sense, is that trauma, and the connection between trauma and our ego, can sometimes feel as if they have a life of their own in our being. They seek their own survival in any way that they can, which often boils down to keeping us as slaves to their selfish purposes, conspiring to drive away everything that we hold dear in life, keeping our dreams far away from us, unhealthy patterns, to kick us when we are down, inflate our ego when we are up... If there is anything about the idea of the devil, then our trauma, our viruses, and the ego that gets created from it as a sort of secondary consciousness, is as close to the devil as it gets.

And after trauma, and the various ills in our world, comes the inevitable discussion on those kinds of people that help to create much of it, from childhood all the way into adulthood...

Narcissistic Woes on a Planetary Scale...

"How starved you must have been that my heart became a meal for your ego..." – **Amanda Torroni**

Something rotten this way cometh...

Narcissism, oh my!

Let me take a few moments to reflect...

So, narcissism is generally considered as sucking, there, done.

No, seriously, the evils we must fight against in our world just to find a little peace and happiness can seem like mountains to move at times. I'm thinking that if all narcissism and similar traits be removed from our world (and the trauma/fears stemming from them), then maybe that is the great "cure" we are all waiting for. Really, once you start understanding the full implications of it, and the domino effect throughout generations, well, again, our notions of "devil" and "Satan", not so far away.

But, I am not saying to go out to your nearest narcissist and call him/her the devil incarnate, no matter how therapeutic that can be. We **all** have some of those traits within us, so if you did point your finger at someone, you'd have to twist your wrist back in your direction also. We can be so afraid of being hurt sometimes, of being vulnerable, of hurting others, a lot of reasons can contribute to make us behave in selfish ways, closed off, but yes, some people have so much more of it than others, and that is what we must all work on to reduce, just be careful of judgments.

So in these next few sections I will focus on the so called "dark" personality traits, including the famous "narcissist" which is getting a lot of attention these days, and for good reason, so it is worth getting into. For a long time people have understood just how bad narcissism can be in our society, the devastating impacts those traits and behaviors have in the world at large. But now people are finally cluing in, they are at long last bringing it down to a personal level, the extent to which narcissism can affect them in their personal lives and relationships, connecting the dots of how much suffering narcissism, and narcissists, can bring into their daily existence.

The Worst Plague?

The amount of abuse and trauma caused by narcissism (and other dark traits) is possibly the worst plague we have ever known, and not just directly, but also by the suffering of their victims and how they go about casting that pain into the world.

Here's a quote that pretty much sums it up:

> *"The narcissist devours people, consumes their output, and casts the empty, writhing shells aside..."* – **Sam Vaknin**

Sam Vaknin is an author, PhD in philosophy and physics, and has focused a lot of his work on narcissism. He was actually diagnosed as having **NPD** (Narcissist Personality Disorder) in his younger years, then changed his life path and sought to understand NDP at a deeper level, so he knows what it's about. He says that people with NPD basically live in their "false self", and while they are associated with those false selves, they cannot be healed as they are not existing as "real people", just reflections.

53

PART 1: A Journey to Emotional Maturity, a New Era to Unfold...

Which is what I get into in regards to the Ego, and as long as people are fully associated with it, such as narcissists, healing is not possible, nor is love or compassion. To heal, we must first realize we are living *as* our Ego, then have the courage to break down those barriers, then do the real work to heal and overcome our trauma and conditioning. I used this quote and example, but there are countless others who share similar views, all the way back to antiquity, as with **Narcissus**, who was so in love with his own image, his reflection, an image we can substitute for our inner Ego or false self. Again, we have been dealing with these same issues for a very, very long time, and still we struggle to have better answers, and also a better way of applying the solutions on a global scale. We keep repeating the same mistakes, everyone keeps focusing on all sorts of things, other than what is truly important, and well...

Back to narcissism and those other dark traits.

First (well, not quite first, but you know), when you start reading into what actually makes a narcissist a narcissist (and associated dark personalities), you might suddenly feel a knot starting to form deep in your being and think "oh my, is he describing *me*?", and if you don't, maybe you should... Anyway, no worries, we all have some, and if you think you are devoid of it, check again, your narcissism might be playing tricks on you. And also, people that seek a healthier path tend to be overly sensitive and put too much emphasis on their own flaws, and are generally very concerned of how they might hurt those around them, so you might lean towards being too hard on yourself, identifying too readily to what you read that could be considered bad, or evil. And second, again, we all have a bit of narcissism, no one is completely loving and selfless. But some people rate much higher than others, and those are the ones we need to be careful of dealing with. And anyone on a healing path that wants more out of their lives, hoping for a great and beautiful story instead of the "run of the mill" kind of existence would do well to know the difference.

"No matter how socially skilled an extreme narcissist is, he has a major attachment dysfunction. The extreme narcissist is frozen in childhood..." – **Samuel Lopez de Victoria**

This quote drives home the notions of trauma I relate to, which often goes back to childhood, and how the more trauma we have, the more we get pulled into various anti-social traits. The more trauma, the more dysfunctional conditioning, the bigger our Ego, the less present we get, the less loving, the more we live a life of illusions in which we are the only master of ceremonies around. Which describes narcissists very well.

Narcissists will always try to pull you into their mind games, into their dark territory where they can control the details. It's like inviting you into their house of smoke and mirrors, and trying to conform you to their design, to fit into the specific slot they want you to be in, to become. A lover, a friend, an adversary, a victim, or a resource to exploit, depending on what they need to feel good about themselves, what character they need you to play as if creating their own movie version of life. **To develop E.M. is to see through their games**, to see and feel the intent behind their words, behind their false façade. And not just with narcissists, but everyone else as well. That can save you from a ton of misery down the road, to not have to spend years with people to find out about them, how selfish, or kind, they actually are. Some people can appear very nice, even though far from it, and some people appear cold and distant, but are actually so compassionate. Most people need a lot of time to figure that stuff out of others, dismissing potentially awesome relationships, and favoring the glitz of narcissism.

E.M. will guide you through the chaos in a much shorter period of time, that is the value of the "emotional sight" you gain from developing it. In many of our interactions, some people just like to cause misery, they'll ask you about the promotion you applied for, not out of caring, but to gloat if you fail, they'll ask you about your recent relationship hoping that it didn't work out. But yet, some people will ask the same questions, but with a caring intent, wouldn't you like to easily tell them apart? To see in their eyes the truth, to know who you can trust with your heart, and who you can't. All those interactions, filtering out automatically from your environment those that don't value your well being, that is possible only with E.M..

The effects of people with ill intents in your environment can be like having an invisible person causing you harm, like rubbing sand paper on your shoulder. You feel pain somewhere, yet you don't see the source of it. We all have them, at work, friends, friends of friends, family, even in our romantic relationships. To grow in E.M. is **shedding light on those situations**, to finally see that person rubbing you with sand paper, to feel the irritation for what it is, their deceit and ill intents are now clear, what they are doing is no longer invisible to you, and you can then easily put a stop to it. You can feel things for what they are, what feels good, and what doesn't, right as it is happening. Yes, it can be hurtful to see in the eyes of someone that they just want to cause pain to you, but best to face that truth than the invisible repercussions. Becoming emotionally mature, to become an *Emotional Adult*, is to understand that humans are complicated, multi-faceted creatures, and many would prefer seeing you fail than to succeed, as it reminds them of their own failures and for a host of other reasons.

That is a reality we must all contend with.

Okay, so it might appear as though I am specifically targeting narcissists as the evil of this world... Though it is not necessarily narcissists themselves I am talking about, but the narcissistic traits within them, and us. So keep in mind that I use narcissism in a "catch-all" kind of way, just as with trauma.

I believe that if there is any real threat to the survival of our species, it has to do with the amount of narcissism and associated traits we have within each and every one of us. It is what makes us most selfish, greedy, violent and overall very anti-social, meaning our needs come way before the needs of anyone else, and to the extreme, even the needs of their own children and spouse are of little importance to a diagnosed narcissist.

The more materialistic, competitive and fearful our world becomes, the more we tend to become individualistic and narcissistic. Along with that, an increase in wars, conflict, terrorism, depression, various emotional and psychological disorders, drug use both medical and illicit, and an overall loss of hope. Suffice to say, there is a good reason why narcissism is part of **The Dark Triad**, it is indeed a terrible darkness to live in, and one that hangs over all of humanity.

The darker people become within themselves, the darker our whole world becomes.

As Within, so Without...

Developing into emotional maturity is pulling away from those dark traits, not just of our trauma, which actually compounds the effects of those narcissistic traits within us, but to follow a path that leads us to all those things that are of love. That is the legacy that everyone working on emotional maturity can leave for the future of humanity. That is "The Great Battle", the tug of war within everyone, a bit more selfish and narcissistic, or a bit more loving and compassionate. Every day we make decisions that pull us one way or the other. It can be quite difficult to understand what goes on, how the little details, the little decisions we make accumulate to one side or the other. Some things are quite evident, but many are not.

PART 1: A Journey to Emotional Maturity, a New Era to Unfold...

"The world is a dangerous place to live, not because of the people who are evil, but because of the people who don't do anything about it..." – **Albert Einstein**

Every night as we go to sleep, our whole being goes through a reconciliation process, what we experienced through the day, knowledge, skills, and the balance between our own good and evil also gets done, the ultimate daily accounting process. Then we wake up the next morning, a little bit more inclined to follow one path, or the other. All of it contributes to a sort of universal balance sheet, for every individual, and for humanity as a whole, to a more loving nature, or, not so much...

WHAT TO LOOK FOR: To give you a better idea, here are some of the most common traits associated with narcissism. Again, keep in mind that we all have some of it, the idea is not to judge, but to understand, and know what to do to lessen its impact on you, from yourself, and others:

- Grandiose sense of their own self-importance, and entitlement
- Using your sensitive spots to hurt you, tease you, bullying, relentless sarcasm
- Always turning the blame back onto you, or anyone else
- Must always protect their Ego, their fantasy world
- Thinking there is nothing wrong with them, ever
- Believe they are superior and can only associate with equally superior people
- And expecting to be recognized as superior even without achievements that warrant it
- Take advantage of others to get what they want
- Monopolize conversations and belittle or look down on people they perceive as inferior
- Have an inability or unwillingness to recognize the needs and feelings of others

- Have significant interpersonal problems and easily feel slighted
- React with rage or contempt and try to belittle others to make themselves appear better
- Often demanding of extreme sacrifices and special offerings
- Love is merely an equation to them, not an actual feeling
- Thinking that self-reflection is for weak, or broken, people
- Very arrogant and exploitative, require constant, excessive admiration
- Unwilling to hear of anything they might have done that is hurtful to anyone
- They believe in nothing more than themselves, and the power they can get from their manipulative behaviors

Generally, you can expect a total lack of empathy, lack of compassion, very very selfish, self-serving, self-absorbed, they can be quite charming which should be a "plus", but they develop this charm to hide the yuck that is underneath the surface and to ensnare people into their evil lairs where they devour their, huh, moving on...

Keep in mind that some good traits might appear narcissistic at times, such as high self-esteem, self-confidence, self-worth... Not always easy to tell apart from arrogance and conceit, and often narcissists will try to make those that have high self-esteem believe *they* are the ones with the problems, which often takes on the form of gaslighting. That's another plus of emotional maturity, to tell the difference, and to not allow anyone to mess around with our sense of self. We are often quite oblivious to the amount of misery we are actually living in, just like a narcissist has no clue as to what love actually is, and how far away they are from it, until they can manage to pull out of their narcissism and see just how far gone they were. And that goes for all of us, until we step out of the old and gain that fresh perspective, it is almost impossible to see that "old" for how bad it actually was. Well, not *that* bad, I'm not implying we're all living in hell or something like that, but meaning too far away from a dream life, where at least most days we feel like we've made it and experience loving feelings on a regular basis for all, or most.

While I'm on the subject, **Gaslighting**: Emotional and psychological manipulation designed to make you question your memories, your feelings, your sense of reality. It is a very cruel tool used by people with narcissistic and sociopathic traits, often to get control of the subjects, to make them do what they want and hide their selfish manipulations. When you start questioning your sense of self, you become easy to control. Governments and news companies (and advertisers) often use this tactic to make people feel there is always a threat to their imminent safety, to make them always think they want something that they don't, or that they need to "listen and do what they are told" otherwise there will be very bad consequences of some sort. And in more normal interactions, when people say mean things then say stuff like "just teasing", "don't take things so personally", "boy, you sure are sensitive", "don't you have a sense of humor?"... As gaslighting is often used by narcissists it can all sound familiar, and it comes in many flavors, I suggest you look more into it from other sources.

SIDE NOTE: I mentioned the associated dark personalities/traits alongside narcissism, so some clarification is in order; there is an actual thing in psychology called *"The Dark Triad"*, so essentially dark personalities, which are: **Narcissism, Psychopathy, and Machiavellianism**, and even potentially a fourth, **Sadism** as a trait that might not be covered by those first 3 (think of the growing trend of some people to gleefully watch videos of people getting hurt, really badly at times, and there's even a new television show that encourages laughing at people's misery). And there's also a common "mixed" trait people refer to as *Sociopathy,* a disorder rather than a trait unto itself (ASPD, or Anti-Social Personality Disorder, which is more of a spectrum, on a sliding scale). The more we encourage those traits, the more we become narcissistic, simple as that. In some circles it is becoming socially acceptable to be narcissistic, even to aim for, but with that we are basically sending the message that love is dead, and "long live" evil and misery. Some people might make fun of the old notions of good versus evil, but when a parent kills their children, when depression and suicide rates increase, human trafficking, rapes, terrorism, school shootings... How can those things not be called evil, and whatever compels people to commit those acts within them, as evil also? If anyone would laugh at those, well, we know very well what kind of individuals we are dealing with.

And believe it or not, there is also *"The Light Triad";* (does Star Wars come to mind?) which are **Katianism** (treating people for who they are, instead of as tools to our ends), **Humanism, and Faith in Humanity.** But hey, this isn't a textbook or dissertation, which is why I have simplified it to mostly using narcissism as a catch all term meaning pretty much all the bad/dark traits bunched together. For *The Light Triad,* I generally refer to as anything loving and compassionate, and the healing path as what inches us along from the Dark Triad to the Light Triad. Again, if you think this sounds a lot like the universe old idea of good versus evil, well, it is as close at it gets, that is what we have been, and are still, fighting for. Trauma, suffering, greed, corruption, dishonesty, all of it is caused by our dark traits (fueled by trauma), and serves to make that part of us even more powerful. Then we must fight against it once we learn how much of a negative influence it can be in our lives, and for planet wide repercussions.

That is the spiritual quest, to love again, fully. Yesterday it was good and evil, today it's love and narcissism, but deep down it's all the same, just as it has always been.

All of this might seem like quite a stretch for those that are simply looking for some basic stuff on emotional intelligence, but as I mentioned, this book goes way beyond the basics, as I believe the basics will pretty much get us nowhere. Like expecting a few showers to fill up a wooden barrel that has more holes in it than a good Swiss cheese. The holes need to be fixed up first, the cracks between the slats mended, the gunk removed from the bottom for the water to be of any good use, then you can have clean rain water collected to water your garden.

Relationships with Narcissists

Being with a narcissist in a romantic relationship can be a true nightmare, and often we don't even realize it until we wake up from the nightmare years later, only to notice the devastating impact, the big craters they left behind, and all the crap they filled those craters with. And of course narcissism is not just limited to romantic relationships, but friendships, co-workers, bosses, family, neighbors, and even politicians. Narcissism can be very devious, it can come to us in a very charming form, and infiltrate our being to poison us from the inside. Many people will relate to this, as everyone has encountered those traits in others, and themselves. A little bit of narcissism can be dealt with, but a lot, it can seem like death to us, it's as if **it kills our sense of self,** like, literally, really... I've had to work hard to rebuild mine, and as long as your sense of self is not very strong, you are prone to either being a further victim of narcissists, or in danger of becoming one yourself. Growing in Emotional Maturity, and building up your *Emotional Immune System*, you learn how to first spot narcissism, not just narcissists themselves, but the traits and behaviors as they come your way, and avoid them, deflect them, and prevent them from affecting, and infecting, you. We can easily become traumatized from the ill effects and abuse from people who have little control over their dark traits, and other than your own personal healing, learning how to avoid and manage those traits in yourself and others might be the most important factor for E.M..

What makes our journey more difficult, is that narcissists are not only *not* interested in anyone's emotional and psychological growth, they will vehemently work against it. If they allow you to grow emotionally and spiritually, then you will no longer tolerate their abuse, or I should say, you will now be able to actually see the abuse/manipulation for what it is, and see how much their self is created by an illusionary ego, an image instead of a human being, so essentially, to see through their bullshit.

"Since narcissists deep down feel themselves to be faultless, it is inevitable that when they are in conflict with the world they will invariably perceive the conflict as the world's fault..."
– M. Scott Peck

Seems like that is how life is, either you accept to live in your Ego (becoming more narcissistic), or you do everything that you can to support love and compassion (like healing and increasing your E.M.), or you get lost somewhere in between, becoming more vacant and depressed, drifting, a victim to be exploited. **As if the universe will not tolerate those who do not choose sides** (consider Napoleon Hill's book: *Outwitting the Devil*) as if we *have* to decide, and do so willingly and with "open eyes", meaning you must know what you are choosing, and why. If you don't choose, then you will tend to drift down the abyss, ripped to shreds by the massive black hole of death, as you are not aiming for the light, for love, then you have nothing to hold on to.

And unfortunately, narcissism can be very "catchy": Sarcasm, enjoying watching people "failing" or getting hurt in videos or in life, the corporate mentality of "dog eat dog", the strongest survive, pressure sales, Wall Street, stock markets, traders, creditors... All help to increase narcissism. People patting themselves on the back for how "ruthless" or nasty they can be, others encouraging them, exploiting the weaknesses of people, enjoying the win, even though to have that win, countless people lost a great deal along the way. Congratulations, you just became the #1 at this or that, all you had to do was being cut-throat to your co-workers, your competitors, to sell shoddy products, to not pay half of your distributors, to deprive yourself of any personal life, to alienate your friends and family, sure, congratulations indeed...

One more narcissist in our world negatively affecting everyone around, and making themselves to be a narcissistic example to their children and those around them. Even amongst friends, we often encourage narcissism more than love and kindness, as narcissism is easy, but for love, for compassion, we need to have strength, we need to allow ourselves to be vulnerable, to care. Too much work for many, or too scary, yet at the same time, those same people crave those loving things in ways they can hardly imagine. And they think they can have it both ways, but life doesn't work like that. For every morsel you feed the narcissistic traits within you, you starve love in equal measure, your being becomes less capable of flowing with love, and all associated traits and feelings dry up like a desert river after years of drought, from the paucity of caring attention and good will.

"Love doesn't die a natural death. Love has to be killed, either by neglect or narcissism..." – **Frank Salvato**

So yes, it can be a load to take on, to comprehend narcissism, in ourselves and others, to face those realities, the truth that is often harsh and deflating. But it is so important to understand what narcissism is, and the associated Dark Triad, all those life sucking dark personality traits and behaviors that we can all have, and how to avoid the ones that are most infected by those aphotic diseases, to ban them from our lives, well, at least keep them at arms length. The more we do that, the more they will have to at some point look at themselves with more scrutiny, and hopefully realize the extent of their aberrations in life. Narcissists do not do well when they don't have non-narcissists to control and manipulate, to feed off of. Just like vampires can't exist if they only have other vampires around them.

The Darkened Skies of the Triads

To think there are people who actually glorify themselves for their dark traits, for being conniving and cunning, controlling and manipulative, and enjoying all the poison fruits of their Machiavel labor. There are many books out there that exemplify narcissistic traits in business and management, politics, and even relationships.

Most of the people who would be reading this book, and have not given up so far, are most likely those serious about developing self-love, to follow a healing path, and are also most likely sensitive people, and sensitive people often fall prey to various forms of insensitive people, narcissists included. Either sensitive people are directly attracted to them because they are reminded of the similar types of abusive relationships from their childhood that feel normal to them, or insensitive people are attracted to sensitive people as they are easy prey, to vent off their abusive natures without much resistance.

"Relationships with narcissists are held in place by hope of a 'someday better,' with little evidence to support it will ever arrive..." – **Ramani Durvasula**

So, again, for anyone on the healing journey, be advised that it is best to avoid these types, at least the stronger ones, to learn how to identify them, and steer clear. They can really mess up your relationship to your feelings, your ability to love yourself, and quite frankly mess up all the most important elements of your life. It is best to leave them fighting against one another instead, maybe then they will eventually learn just how much pain they can cause, or completely exhaust themselves from the perpetual fighting for their lives, as drowning victims in their own sorrows, just make sure you don't offer yourself up as their life preserver.

IMPORTANT NOTE: And again, to be fair, I should mention that I don't believe people are born narcissists (or any of those dark traits), anyone. Maybe unless they experienced physical brain trauma in their mother's womb that would make them that way, from a blow, or chemicals like drugs and alcohol during pregnancy, but don't quote me on that, I don't think such data even exists. But I would say narcissists don't *ask* to be like that, meaning narcissists are "made" in childhood for the most part, most likely from their parents/environment. So you know, being kind and compassionate towards them, but not tolerating their abuse, can be a hard line at times to manage, but, something to think about. They are most likely a product of their environment, and we should not treat those behaviors as if people become like that of their own free will (same with your own level of narcissism). They do to a certain extent, but most of it is programming that is very difficult to overcome. But at the same time, we gotta do what we gotta do. Like having compassion for a murderer, for the often difficult life they have had themselves, but at the same time, needing to punish them for their crime, and prevent them from killing again.

All of that put together is why I relate to narcissism and related traits more akin to living from our animal predispositions. And that our human nature is more related to love and compassion, to seek community and engagement, to consider the long term welfare of our species. And that might be the battle within we all struggle with, **our human nature struggling to overcome the animal nature we've evolved from**, our soul trying to express itself through the remnants of our animal ancestors which are all those negative, self-serving and violent traits and behaviors.

So, in a way you can think of a "full" narcissist as an emotional caveman, **human 1.0**, the "missing link" between our animal ancestors and the future loving, enlightened and compassionate human that has outgrown all those "evil", animal traits. A bridge between two realities, and we are in the middle of this process of change, of evolving to a new era. We are slowly stepping out of our caves, out of hoarding resources and violent/controlling tendencies, and trying to build up a stronger and healthier race that will seek community and compassion as a foundation, to build something that we can all look up to with great satisfaction. Seems like our physical bodies are evolving more rapidly than our internal psychological and emotional states, creating the illusion that we are doing "good enough", but there is so much more room to grow, we need to see that.

"Narcissism is voluntary blindness, an agreement not to look beneath the surface..." – **Sam Keen**

Survival of the fittest should no longer be about brute strength, the ones with the most resources, manipulation and control. We are not animals anymore, and it is time we leave those behaviors behind, in the caves of our ancestors where they belong. Humanity should strive towards togetherness, sharing, compassion, higher values and morals. Emotional maturity can take us there. **We need a new definition of what it is to be human**, and to have the courage to make the changes in our societies to make that new reality happen. Narcissism and its associated anti-social traits are much more animal like than human like, in terms of how people behave, the goals they set for themselves and their overall outlook on life.

We need to figure out how to root out those traits once and for all if we want our world to change for the better, and the next sections are all about that.

And now, after all this talk about dark things and yucking in the mud of our primitive ancestors, I need to take a break, a shower, or a bath, then come back with something lighter, how does that sound to you?

PART 1.2: "L'Essentiel est Invisible pour les Yeux"

Well, that was a lot to take in!

But there are no "one stop shops" for developing into a full grown, emotionally mature human being. Remember, you are worth all the effort you put into yourself, much more than you can realize right now.

To change things up and set a different tone, consider this:

"On ne voit bien qu'avec le coeur. L'essentiel est invisible pour les yeux..."

This is a well known quote from the book "***Le Petit Prince***" by **Antoine de Saint-Exupéry**.

Translated, it means that we can only see well with our heart, what is most important is invisible to our eyes, a sentiment I share.

So to develop the capacity to "see" with our heart is essential to not only see ourselves and the world for what they are, but also to develop higher E.M.. That is what this section will be about, how to develop that special "sight", and understanding what we need to do to get there.

Maybe that is why your life isn't as good as what you would like it to be, like the majority of people? Not because of who you are and what you are capable of or not, but because of who you *see* yourself as, and your inability to find the best path that you can follow through all the invisible obstacles that keep tripping you up, and the parts of you that go unnoticed in the background, parts that you need to get to that great life you keep dreaming about.

When we can start seeing and feeling clearly, all the situations we find ourselves in, our relationships, our whole timeline, us, then we start to make much better decisions for ourselves. So to see with our physical eyes is one thing, **but to "see and feel" with our heart** adds a whole new dimension to our existence. Then all of those barriers, our fears, conditioning, all become visible to us for what they are, then we can tackle them one by one. Healing our wounds, our trauma, is an important part of this process, as it burdens our heart to such an extent that we cannot see or feel anything from it, or very little, not enough to make better decisions for our future.

And always keep in the back of your mind how in the end, all of this is related to your capacity to love, and be loved.

Seeing, and Feeling, from the Eyes of your Heart

"Change can be hard. It requires no extra effort to settle for the same old thing. Auto-pilot keeps us locked into past patterns. But transforming your life? That requires courage, commitment, and effort. It's tempting to stay camped in the zone of That's-Just-How-It-Is. But to get to the really good stuff in life, you have to be willing to become an explorer and adventurer..." – **John Mark Green**

As we are moving along to more practical applications, what we can actually *do* to heal and develop E.Q., and E.M., think of self-reflection as the first step to take on this journey, as without it, almost everything within you will go unnoticed and remain the same. And if you are reading this book, chances are you don't want things to remain the same, only people living in fear of themselves are willing to accept less than stellar lives, and they usually want to stay well enough away from books that aim to change their inner status quo, that seek to direct light to the things they refuse to look at, to become true explorers of their inner jungles.

Without self-reflection, we are all more or less like sailboats without rudders, sailing in the darkness, adrift in a sea of dreadful sameness, aimlessly banging into one another. Our physical eyes can only see a minuscule portion of the world around us. 99 percent of everything in existence, and then some, cannot be seen directly, including all the emotional and mind based stuff that goes on inside each and everyone one of us. And to think that most of our reality gets created by things we can't even bring into consciousness, that is something I find difficult to accept. To limit yourself only to what is visible, to accept your feelings and emotions as they are without question, **is to dismiss the majority of what life could**

be for you, and also to dismiss your own truer self in the process. Your perception of who you are, and what you are capable of, is quite limited if you don't figure out a better way of organizing your internal world, developing a better capacity to manage your thoughts and emotions, and to get over your own obstacles that keep you grounded in the same old stuff day after day, the humdrum of being lost at sea.

To be able to self-reflect in any appreciable way, to actually achieve some results out of it, it is necessary to develop a better method of "internal" sight. Like having x-ray vision, to see all the way through yourself, and others too. To see and feel with the heart, past all the crap we normally contend with, and project. Some of it we know, and a lot we don't. To refer to this sight, of seeing life, people, ourselves, through the eyes of our heart, I felt I should give it a proper name. And since it is not only related to seeing, but also feeling, I have called it developing a better pair of emotional glasses, so those "**E-Glasses**" I talked about earlier. Basically, to see and feel when people are lying to us, what they fear, what they hide, and what you hide from yourself, the trauma, repressed stuff, subconscious desires, the parts stuck in the past. And to be able to see all the good stuff as well, for what it is, even the things people might be reluctant to share, to see beauty in familiar things, in simple gestures, in everyday life. It is kind of like another super power that we can develop, and to help us ward off those "evil" narcissists and Dark Triads gang members! Or at least see through their tricks and manipulations.

We all have a basic pair of E-Glasses as we all have a certain capacity to feel our emotions and the emotions of others. Think about these E-Glasses as related to E.Q.: The lower your E.Q., the more your E-Glasses don't work very well, as if they are cracked, dirty, oily, and the lenses have a very limited capacity to see colors as they are, opaque filters obstruct much of what you see (like that busted up telescope). Everything is muted, bland, and not only is your emotional perception very limited, you keep getting emotions and feelings mixed up with one another.

What does this look like? For one, low E.Q./immature people tend to have a very limited control over their emotions, and also tend to have a limited expression of them, which is often mainly dominance, fear, violence, greed, all those lower types of negative emotions, much like prey/predator animals. Their E-Glasses can't do much more than that. And think about these E-Glasses as not only allowing you to see and feel the emotions and feelings of a situation, **but also express them**, they are all the same and tied into one another. So your E-Glasses are not just about understanding emotions, feeling them, but also expressing them, expressing the "truer" you. Think about someone who has a fear of public speaking, once on a stage their various emotions can actually block the function of speech, so their E-Glasses have certain filters that turn public speaking into something terrifying, they might subconsciously see/feel the audience as projections of their fears, their trauma, which we often do, fears of failure and such.

So maybe E-Glasses is not quite adequate to fully explain what their function is, but you get the point. Our various wounds, fears, trauma, programming, and generally low abilities in E.Q. block our lives in many more ways than we understand. Try to think of these E-Glasses and all the ways they become dysfunctional both from emotional and psychological issues as actual impairments that you must fight against everyday of your life, kind of like energetic barriers that block and misrepresent many things inside of you, and how you perceive things outside of your own self.

So these E-Glasses are not just about seeing and feeling, but also about getting a different, deeper, more mature and understanding perspective on everything, including all elements of your own life, and yourself. They are what will help you see and feel life from your heart, instead of your mind or your pain/ego, and then to recreate it using much healthier elements.

"Love takes off masks that we fear we cannot live without and know we cannot live within..." – **James Baldwin**

A whole new Perspective on Life

Developing higher E.M. is about that, getting a whole new perspective of yourself and others beyond what people are actually sharing, what lies behind the words they use, and the motives and intents of their behavior, and yours. Without it, you more or less use your brain to try to figure out everything, and not only is the brain very ill suited for such a task as figuring out if that blind date is a serial rapist or the nicest guy on the planet, but it adds a tremendous load on it in many other ways, and also it just isn't made to interpret feelings, it burdens the hell into it.

Example of a person with lower E.M./Dysfunctional E-Glasses, from your perspective: You are walking down a sidewalk, people up ahead are having a discussion, you pass them, and a few feet ahead you trip a bit, and at the same time you hear the word "stupid" from one of the people. You get all upset, mad, you think they called you stupid for tripping. You carry that anger with you to work, your boss notices, and your chances of getting any advance diminishes a bit more. As you have low E.M. (in this example only of course:), you are prone to see the negative in things, and carry that kind of behavior everywhere you go. With very imperfect E-Glasses, you see the world more like with tunnel vision, and a very blurry tunnel at that. You have completely blocked out the first part of the conversation, even if you heard it with your ears, your mind dismissed it as unimportant, as with low E.M., we tend to focus on the hurt, instead of the good. The first part of what came before in their conversation was "I think that show is so stupid", and of course, people usually emphasize the word stupid in that context. But because of your history, because of low self-esteem and whatever else contributed to your low E.M., you naturally project your pain all around you, and re-create all sorts of situations to match the specific wounds and trauma you have experienced in either your childhood, or through adult relationships and situations.

We all do this more or less, and the more wounds and trauma you have, the lower the E.M., the worst your "sight" and perception will be. Everything becomes about you, you take things personally, you see threats everywhere, and there are *many* of those "false threats" when our E-Glasses are badly damaged, or I should say we *interpret* many situations as a threat, even when no threat is present, and even the fears of rejection and abandonment are seen as threats to our existence. You live in fear, in conditioning, and you get triggered by all sorts of things, most of them not real, or not intended in the way you perceive them. **Life is very bleak and limited for people with very dysfunctional E-Glasses.** Just imagine actually taking a pair of normal glasses, cracking the lenses, putting dirt on them, adding layers of colored filters, until you can barely see anything, all blurry. People become distorted, monster like, everything is literally darker, your boss makes you think of someone who abused you as a child, you don't clearly see your children as your own, they become "things" that bother you (as your hearing and other senses are also affected), your spouse suddenly reminds you of a childhood bully. This is not an exaggeration, people with low E.Q./E.M. keep interpreting everything around them based on their painful past experiences. Or projecting the good experiences on bad situations, such as projecting the feelings of a childhood sweetheart, the only person they ever thought they could care about, on that abusive narcissist they are having a blind date with, and those broken E-Glasses will get them into an abusive relationship, many years of additional suffering for them.

With proper E-Glasses, your "tripping" on the sidewalk could have made you notice a 20$ bill under a newspaper dispenser instead of focusing on what those people were saying, that found money making you happy, but before you put it in your pocket, you ask the people if they dropped it, they say no, you carry on, happier. You notice children playing in the park, the leaves blowing in the wind, you get to work happy, your boss notices, etc, etc... This is not fiction, that is how life is. This example might be a bit exaggerated, but it happens, more or less like that. And what compounds the issues, is that our physical eyes are very blind to what is truly going on, they see people as people, all more or less the same, while our internal world can be so distant from our external reality.

In all kinds of ways life leaves us short of satisfied, abused, traumatized, and little by little all that pain that we carry, the regret, the shame, the longing for better days, all leave their scars on our E-Glasses, all create dysfunctional programming that remains until we overcome it.

Developing the Capacity for Self-reflection, and Being Alone

As mentioned in the last section, self-reflection is a very important, nay, crucial aspect of developing higher E.M.. So it makes sense that those with the lowest E.M. are the ones least likely to engage in it, and the most likely to never grow out of their trauma and emotional immaturity. What makes it scary for them is that the more trauma and wounds they carry, often means the most abusive and traumatizing their past to face, and the more imperfections within them to overcome. One of life's many "unfairnesses", not to say that all people with low E.Q. get like that from abuse and trauma, some simply didn't have much of a chance to develop it, but it is still an important contributor, and one that can mostly be reversed.

"To dare to live alone is the rarest courage; since there are many who had rather meet their bitterest enemy in the field than their own hearts in their closets..."
– Charles Caleb Colton

Again, loving something you don't really understand is quite difficult, especially yourself. There might seem to be a discrepancy in between the ideas of "not loving what we don't understand" and "unconditional love", but in actuality, developing unconditional love requires a very thorough knowledge of ourselves and other people. **To love unconditionally is to know all, and to love anyway**. That's the main reason why it is extremely difficult to love unconditionally, something most people can only hope to achieve a small amount of, if blessed and dedicated in their journey.

About being alone, but not lonely: Self-reflection and being alone go together, and it goes without saying that a person that does not love themselves has a very low tolerance for being alone, and with that low tolerance self-reflection becomes very difficult... But, I said it anyway, so I guess it doesn't go *without* saying. Does anyone use that expression and *not* say what they intended to say? "It goes without saying", then a long blank...

Hmm, seems like a redundant saying come to think of it...

So, then, if a person does not love themselves very much, they will not be able to stand their own company, they will always need distractions, people around them, television, or drugs and alcohol, anything to not "be" with themselves at any substantial level. People with high E.M. can be alone without feeling lonely as much, people with low E.M. will pretty much always feel lonely when alone and without distractions as they have difficulty tolerating their own company, and even with others.

And that leaves us in a conundrum, as self-reflection requires a certain amount of self-love, and self-love requires a certain amount of ability to be alone in our own company to self-reflect, and self-reflection requires a certain amount of self-love, so it goes back in circles, like a double catch 22, a catch 44, or 22+22, or a catch 484, or, anyway, something like that...

"In solitude, the soundless dialogue which the soul holds with herself finally becomes audible..." – **Jennifer Stitt**

So, to break that pattern takes courage, and courage requires higher E.M., and then we start to realize why it can be so difficult for people to get a head start in all of this. But we must if we want our lives to get better. So, in the beginning, you can expect some pain, some suffering, some loneliness, as you develop higher E.M. and pursue a healing journey. Most people seek to avoid their inner pain, so they just amble on in their 9-5, and their dreams remain in the back of their closets alongside various mementos, photos, and souvenirs. Ah, something to reminisce once every few years, the "better" days, the few that we remember as good, to keep us in the belief that the other forgettable 364 days of each year were worth living (365 in some cases), to at least have those few we can recount to ourselves in our golden years... Okay, I have to admit, that might be a slight lapse in sarcasm, sorry, I was raised in it, dipped into that big vile well growing up, and I haven't quite shaken off all the oily sludge yet, pardon me. But I now remember some of my own words; to be kind, to forgive, take a deep breathe, and let go...

I feel better now, thanks for your concern!

Carrying Forth

So you can understand how important it is to develop that capacity to be alone, otherwise if you always flee from your own thoughts, your feelings, you will never know what lies beneath them, which is often the trauma that we have forgotten, neglected, or repressed (and all sorts of other little things that go bump in the night, like that time you cheated on your spouse, or when you lied to your boss, your fear of spiders, fudging on your taxes, assorted regrets...). That is what people run away from most, their own shadows, the stuff in their closet, those subconscious shoe boxes that contain not the cherished souvenirs of their past, but all the things that have fallen into various states of disrepair. If you want to properly face all that stuff, you will have a very hard time doing that when surrounded by distractions or with other people, unless the point is specifically for that, such as support groups or therapy.

Oh, just thought of something, what is self-reflection anyhow?

From Wikipedia: *Human self-reflection is the capacity of humans to exercise introspection and to attempt to learn more about their fundamental nature and essence.*

So, self-reflection is reflecting on the deeper parts of yourself, how you interact with others, going through your day, your conversations, your past, and looking at yourself as from the eyes of an observer.

Consider this famous quote from **Socrates**:

"An unexamined life is not worth living..."

A tad drastic, but yet even two thousand years ago people already knew how important this was (and much further back still), yet that wisdom is getting lost somewhere in between social media, all the negative and fearful news, low attention spans, and people's individual quest for fame and fortunes, the many ways we get pulled deeper into our Egos. For many, life simply has become too complicated and busy to "bother" with examining their lives. But, as it is the only path to building self-love, they have very little clue to what they discard of themselves as they focus on those external goals that keep them living in the material world only, not acknowledging the emotional and psychological stuff that accumulates in the background. Mid-life crisis, heart attacks and burn outs waiting to happen.

I can't say that I blame them though, even if blaming them could not only be therapeutic but might be an incentive for them to give it a shot, as the more people there are who refuse to admit even to themselves their impairments, and do all sorts of things to avoid them, well, the more our whole world becomes a reflection of those lies and deceits. But, to set a better example, I understand why you do it, all of you, and why there might still be some stuff I have not admitted to myself yet either despite my many attempts to exorcise all the stuff dwelling in forgotten places. We all should give ourselves a great big hug right now, and tell ourselves "I love you, you dysfunctional, imperfect, but doing the best you can person I am forced to spend my entire life with!".

And you can take *that* to the bank, a trip well worth the detour!

DISCLAIMER: With all this talk about being alone, I don't mean to isolate yourself, to become a loner, and to keep everything hidden, that is not what is intended by self-reflection and the capacity to be alone. Sharing your deeper wounds and trauma can be very therapeutic when done with caring people. In fact, I encourage people to be more open with what they have experienced. Developing the capacity to be alone doesn't mean to *stay* alone always, it means **to be able**

to be alone for periods of time, without distractions, without avoiding your inner pain, and without always running away from your fears. Part of the *"raison d'être"* of this book is to help people understand they are *not* alone in their suffering, to be able to face it within themselves without shame, and also to know many others are in the same situation, if not most, or even all. Take only one type of trauma, stemming from sexual abuse in children: Statistics can vary greatly, from 1 in 3, to 1 in 10 children having experienced sexual abuse, depending on the source, and depending on whether we are talking about girls or boys. We can normalize it to around 20% in total for the sake of this example, which seems to be the consensus. That number is staggering on a global scale, and girls generally represent maybe 80% of the victims. If 20% of all children have experienced sexual abuse of some form (and most likely more), that represents about 1.5 billion people on this planet, and most feel shameful about it, to the point of not mentioning it, keeping it within themselves like a tumor that never gets healed, never receives love, parts of them that never get hugged, or soothed... **Potentially 1.5 billion people that think they are alone in their suffering**, just for that type alone. That is sad indeed, and most do not share their pain because they feel there is something wrong with *them*, and they live their whole lives concealing that shame. Please, by all means, you are not alone, you are not wicked nor defective for what others have done to you. So, by being alone, I don't mean keep all of your stuff to yourself, but at least take some time to look at all of it on your own (which can still include therapy), then know you are *not* alone, even though you should first face it on your own terms, then try to grow the courage to face the world with it. It is not easy, but it can be done. Again, just for this type of trauma, the world suffers a great deal more than anyone can imagine, it might be the single most important source of pain for humanity, and the silence of it hurts us all. If we all spoke out about it, to not keep it full of shame and guilt, well, we could experience a tremendous healing spurt the size of the moon, and that is a dream worth having!

I would like to take this time to congratulate all of you people who have managed to not fall into a big heaping mess of pain and suffering, for all the trauma and wounding you have suffered, and are still carrying. You are a testament to how much humans can keep going despite the immense burdens of the past they might be carrying, all while keeping a straight face, doing your job, raising your own family in the best way that you can. You, taking a sip of coffee in your favorite coffee shop, on your sofa or in your bed, taking a bath, or sunning yourself on a beach, you know who you are, you know what you have lived through, and still you find a way to get out of bed in the morning and face another day. I share this time with you (>^_^)>

Okay, back to the book!)

Considering all of this, if you just start trying to peer deep within yourself right now, like really, *right now*, you might fall a bit short of your goals, what will you try "looking" at? And how could you see anything more than what you might have already seen before reading these few pages, how could you think you would get much better results? And also, to grow the courage to face your deepest wounds doesn't come overnight, you must work on it, care for yourself in the process, it takes time, so be patient while you love yourself through your pain, a little at a time.

Take courage, self-reflection gets much better the more you heal and fix those E-Glasses, to get a different perspective on things, so that eventually you will get results that had so far escaped your grasp.

MEDITATION: This is a great time to consider incorporating a meditation practice in your schedule, start small, maybe once or twice a week, even just 10-15 minutes to begin with. Numerous studies have been done concluding in the many emotional, psychological, and physical benefits of regular meditation. It is practically a must for anyone trying to develop E.M., and it doesn't have to be the classic sitting in lotus position kind of thing, even mindful thinking and feeling anywhere you are can be considered meditation (even when walking to work), the important thing is to start. There are numerous resources online, and several good quality apps available (like *Calm* and *Headspace*), to make it easier to get into the habit of it. I have included several suggestions in the back matter of this book, check them out!

Getting past what is *not* Essential

"It takes courage to love, but pain through love is the purifying fire which those who love generously know. We all know people who are so much afraid of pain that they shut themselves up like clams in a shell and, giving out nothing, receive nothing and therefore shrink until life is a mere living death..." – **Eleanor Roosevelt**

To stop seeing only what you want to see, and to stop feeling only what you want to feel requires courage. And as the quote, if what is essential is invisible to the eyes, then one could surmise that our eyes are very good at only seeing what is *not* essential, which is what we often focus on without knowing how unessential what we are looking at really is.

It makes sense doesn't it?

If you keep looking at yourself and the world around you in the same way, then how can you expect anything to change? If you are in an abusive relationship at home, even just from verbal abuse now and then, but you don't take the time to actually see, or feel, the abuse from a different perspective, as in how it truly affects you, the repercussions of those effects at work, with your boss, with your family, your children. How you might then take that abuse, the hurt and passive aggressive behavior that often comes from it, or the myriad repressed feelings, and then pass those on to your friends, co-workers... If you don't look at all of it for what it is, and how much your life might be diminished by it, how your friends are growing tired of your emotional distance, how your boss passed you up for a promotion, how that made you feel unworthy, lowered your self-confidence, if you refuse to look at all of that, to feel it, process it, then how can things change? And even more so for childhood trauma, which has been affecting you for so long, and been responsible for directing so much of your life to bad situations. All that trauma combining to create a sort of inner self that resembles more a crazed symphony conductor making a terrible mess of your life rather than a loving and caring self that you wish you were.

If you don't work harder on becoming the master of all of your functions, including thoughts, emotions, and feelings, then you can't become the master of your life, the accomplished conductor to your absolutely marvelous symphony, harmonies to make all the world gasp in awe. **If you are not the master of your domain, then of course someone else will take up that position**, someone else will play all, or most, of your inner instruments for you, and make their own music from your soul, to which they will own the copyrights, and you get nada, a few crumbs here and there, that's pretty much it. That doesn't sound like much fun does it? But it happens *all the time*, sorry, take a cue from the music industry. (Yes, I do enjoy allegories and metaphors, yes I do)

For every part of yourself that you have left unexplored, anything you don't understand, that you avoid facing, all those fears, the trauma, the ways your present and past experiences have affected you, all become uncharted waters in your subconscious. And all those parts are up for grabs to anyone who understands them better than you do, or have figured out a way to take advantage of them. That's what narcissists do, they have "a nose" for the openings in your subconscious to manipulate and control you, advertisers home-in on people's repressed desires to sell them stuff, and politicians and news people prey on your fears and trauma to further their agenda and condition you to whatever "reality" they want you to believe in.

MAKING IT WORK: So then, how do we develop a better capacity of sight, to not only see from our physical eyes, but through the eyes of our hearts, and gain that extra perspective?

First, to have the courage to face the pain, the pain that is already within you, and the pain that people might send your way, or you at them. If someone screams at you, don't scream back, tell them that it causes you pain. When someone says mean things, like with sarcasm, don't engage in the sarcasm, or dismiss it, tell them that their comments are hurtful, and why. If someone tries to take advantage of you, tries to make you do things you are not comfortable with, say no, if you are afraid of losing friends, then have faith that if they are good friends, they will respect you for it, if not, then it isn't a friend you are losing, just someone you spend time with and don't really share a good connection. When you feel like crying, go ahead, and try to understand everything that is making you cry at that time. Everything that you do to try to understand your feelings better will help you to see more clearly, every time you tell a person in very plain language when they are being hurtful will also help to increase your understanding of your feelings, to grow in E.M.. If we don't face our internal pain, we become blind to similar pain, and we don't even notice it happening anymore, the more pain, the more blindness, I think you're starting to feel those connections are you not? And it's not just about the painful stuff, the great things also, love, happiness, compassion, to allow yourself to express your full range of feelings.

All the great benefits of a life well examined, peeling the layers one by one, to reveal the *you* that you always knew was there, but got lost somewhere along the way, if not lost, buried under mounds of detritus, detritus that make up the false you. Understand that those initial layers will be the hardest to pry open and to overcome, as they are often the heaviest, and scariest. And as your skills are not so well honed, it can be more difficult and painful. But it gets better with practice, truly, it does, but you need to really, really want it...

"Nothing happens until the pain of remaining the same outweighs the pain of change..." – **Arthur Burt**

So yes, go ahead and think about your best life as your personal perfect symphony to offer to the world, to rejoice in, you as the master conductor of all of your internal parts, and with that, the master of your external world as well (with some reservations of course*). A symphony that you can take all the credit for, and profit from all the riches and glory.

Self-love and healing go a long way baby, get used to it!

*Small print: Yes, some luck, being in the right place and the right time helps, some financial resources, a good network, some time and elbow grease, but you got that, you're smart after all. Love is great, but we need to build up from there, to attract better things, patience and such, eventually your life *will* get better.

MUSICAL INTERLUDE: Here's another song to try out, *The Shape of Us* by **Ian Britt**, think of it as your own little serenade...

You are not your Thoughts, nor your Trauma

Before we get to the next section, I have a few words to share concerning anything you might come to comprehend of yourself through this self-reflection process. When we start seeing ourselves better, all our flaws, our imperfections, the stuff that was done to us, and what we have done, to see all of it in a better light, with better *E-Glasses*, there will be times when you might feel ashamed, embarrassed, feeling guilty, regrets... Through it all, keep in mind that we *all* do things that can make us feel in those ways, we all have experienced things that have made us feel we were bad and deserving of them, even if only subconsciously. What is important is to feel the truth of those feelings, but to not accept them as the "ultimate" truth of *who* we are. **We are not those thoughts, we are not those feelings, nor those experiences**. They come through us as we explore the unexplored within, as we grow the courage to sail on the seas of our subconscious, and to look at all of our life for what it truly was, and is, with better sight and feelings, grounded in truth and reality.

So don't be too hard on yourself, remember to practice being kind and loving, especially in consideration of the next section. Your experiences, and your thoughts, what goes on in your mind, you are not that. You are not a person deserving of abuse, you never were (though some are deserving of punishment, but that topic is too much to explore here). Your mind can be a wild place, even more so when we start triggering repressed pain and memories, and how we might be angry at those people responsible, past and present.

"To realize that you are not your thoughts is when you begin to awaken spiritually..." – **Eckhart Tolle**

So, all those skeletons in the closet that you might dig up, you are not that, you are not the dirt, you are not the smell, you are not the cobwebs nor the spiders, or any related emotions that will come up, keep that in mind, smile, you are awesome!

A Life in Review

Once we understand the importance of self-reflection and the other basic stuff that goes along with it, a major life review can be next on your list.

All of your life, all facets of it, from your earliest memories to your last, especially in relationship to emotions, the good, the bad, and the ugly. But don't get too hung up or discouraged by the use of "major". Keep in mind this is a lifelong process, like eating healthy, not something you get into for a month and then let go, take it in increments. With eating, if you do a one week a year healthy eating thing, then go back to eating chips and donuts as your main meals, your health will suffer the consequences. Same as with emotional and psychological health, and those should be taken much more seriously as your whole life gets built from them. It's not just a spare tire you will get caught up with, but all sorts of missed opportunities, the quality of your relationships will suffer, rejection, career, earning potential, and of course, your capacity for love and happiness.

The recent pandemic is stretching our capacity to maintain the same paths, we can use what we learn about ourselves to make better choices, to understand what isn't working, and what is. To relive all the pains of the past in a new light, with better tools, to free them from your system once and for all. That is how love can come, higher E.M., everything in life will then *feel* better to you. The same things will have an improved flavor, the same difficulties will now seem lighter.

> *"It is not that something different is seen, but that one sees differently. It is as though the spatial act of seeing were changed by a new dimension..."* – **Carl Jung**

Hopefully it is becoming much clearer why a simple "10 step to emotional freedom and increased E.Q." might sound good on paper, and might make a person feel better and help gain a few insights, but in reality, it will hardly put a dent on anyone's true Emotional Maturity level. It is not something you can just get into once in a while, then go back to bad E.Q. habits, any gain will just be lost.

Remember that unconditional love can only be felt in the absolute present, so anything that pulls your thoughts and feelings away from the present, also pulls you further away from the ability to love. The things you have not let go of, attachments, emotional stuff not reconciled, even the multitude of things you have not said, or not allowed yourself to express, or to feel, all those unsaid and unfelt things need to come out, to see the light of day.

The collective history of humanity, all the pain, the wars, the abuse, everything of an emotional nature that is still hanging on to memories, all prevent us from evolving towards a new era, a loving nature, and a loving world. It is all part of developing a new vocabulary, a way of re-telling our story in a much better way, on renewed terms and conditions. We ourselves hold the keys to that path, each and every one of us. It is within our power to change, but the past needs to be let go of, and our present selves need to overcome those things within us that prevents us from letting go, and also to let go of the things that keep attracting those unhealthy cycles into our lives.

Understanding Abuse and Trauma

To understand fully, and to fully love what is understood, that is the journey of a lifetime.

This is a good place to start for a "Life Review", as without *knowing* what we are reviewing, our efforts would fall kind of flat. I have talked a bit about trauma in earlier sections, but it's another one of those topics that can be quite long for anyone that wants to fully understand it, so I'll go a bit more into the mechanics of it here. But of course you don't have to know *everything* about it, and you can always start your review while learning along the way. As trying to understand everything before you begin can be hard or even impossible, and starting before you understand enough also, so a bit of learning, a bit of practice, you'll get the hang of it.

AND A REMINDER: By trauma, I do mean all those imperfections in your system that block love, that hinder your progress to a greater life, those "negative" energies like greed and envy, dysfunctional conditioning, regrets and shame, judgments and such.

I have recently been introduced to the work of **Pete Walker**, I read two of his books *"The Tao of Fully Feeling"* and *"COMPLEX PTSD: From Surviving to Thriving"*, which have helped me to understand abuse and trauma at a deeper level, and to overcome a bit more of it. There are many other great books out there, some of which I mention in other sections. Look into abuse and trauma, especially related to healing relationships if you want to know more about it.

Trauma can be one of those things that people don't want to consider themselves "with", as in traumatized, wounded, but again, we all are. Even though emotional trauma is a universal condition, it doesn't mean *you* are the wound itself. Like if you cut your finger and it gets infected with puss, you are not the puss, you are not the wound, nor the pain. Even if you are wounded, traumatized, injured, this is not who *you* are, same as with your emotional trauma.

We are what we are, and yes we are all traumatized to a certain degree. And probably most childhood trauma has become *complex* over the years, which means it has become associated with all sorts of situations and experiences, people, goals, possessions, and **no longer has one specific point of origin**, which makes it harder to figure out and let go of.

Think of being yelled at over and over again by your mother in very mean ways, a person who you looked up to for compassion and nurturing, a person that is/was also your primary caretaker, someone in authority over you. So you get all sorts of traumatized emotions from the yelling, which become dysfunctionally associated with love, and also with your relationship to authority, and coming from the person responsible for your physical safety and survival, so fears of rejection and abandonment get also mixed in, it can create quite a mess inside of people. A potent mix of wounding happens in those situations, which affect all sorts of our relationships as adults, what we seek in partners, what we run away from, careers, so, *complex* trauma. Getting punched once by a classmate as a 10 year old, not nearly as complex, and might not even become trauma, yet most likely will, but much easier to deal with as a one time thing.

And for **PTSD**, Post Traumatic Stress Disorder: Although it would be a stretch to say we *all* have it, as a clinical "disorder" requires certain specific things, like with "major" depression, you can have quite a bit of depression, without it being *major*, or being very narcissistic, without being all the way to having it as a disorder. So, having trauma, by definition means we also have *post* trauma effects as none of our experiences remain in the present, so they engender repercussions *after* the incident, and it often becomes complex as time goes by.

The reason I mention this is not to confuse you, really, but for the sake that many would never think of checking into "Post Traumatic Stress Disorders" as part of a normal healing journey, or even simple trauma, thinking only war veterans have it, those involved in combat and death. But no, just as so many people suffer from depression without it being major, we all suffer from post traumatic stress, even if we don't have the disorder. And great insights can be had by learning about PTSD, especially when related to the more common applications of it. And even if the "stress" part is low, and might not get the extreme reactions to triggers as some war veterans, we still get triggered, and we still react on it, even if only yelling or crying, or shutting down.

Pretty much everyone can relate to being emotionally triggered now and then, but it is not something we have to accept. Though as long as it remains unhealed, it will create various ill effects inside of us even when not triggered, even when the trauma lies dormant within us.

The Commonality of Abuse

Abuse is much more common than we think it is. There are numerous situations that we do not consider as abuse, but are, and do indeed often cause trauma. Think of something small, like gently rubbing your finger on sandpaper just for the experience of it. It does not feel pleasant, but let's say you do it anyway, as it is only a minor discomfort. Once finished with the sensory experience, you just go on with your day. But for your body, for your finger, that experience was abuse, and it caused trauma to your finger, if only very little, not even enough for you to notice, of feel the after effects. Your skin was "abused", it was deliberately rubbed on a harsh surface just to have that sensation, and even if you don't see the "trauma", it is there. On close inspection you might see the roughness of the skin, where it was once soft. Your skin was in effect traumatized. **As children we face so many similarly abusive situations beyond just the physical**, sometimes of our own accord, oftentimes not. And even though most of the time the physical wounds heal from physical abuse, the emotional wounds often require much more than time to heal. And emotional and psychological trauma usually does not heal on its own over time, unless we actually do something about them, or we find ourselves in good healthy environments where some of the healing can come naturally. And keep in mind that *all trauma negatively affects our E-Glasses*, including all the negative effects from that, which also lowers our E.Q./E.M. (and pulls you more towards narcissism), and generally makes life suck, suck very much, like big time sucking, the kind that leaves you wishing you were born a tree sometimes. (Leaves you, tree...)

"Emotional abuse can leave a victim feeling like a shell of a person, separated from the true essence of who they naturally are. It also leads to a victim feeling tormented and tortured by their own emotions..." – **Lorraine Nilon**

So think of abuse as something that happens to us in the moment that is emotionally, physically, or psychologically painful, and maybe not even perceived as pain, but has a negative impact on us. And trauma is the resulting wounds from the abuse, even if it can be nearly imperceptible at times. A parent that continuously drills into their children that money is the most important factor in life, well that can be abusive to our loving nature, and can have a big negative impact on us. Those are the kinds of battles that go on in people when they reach adulthood, they seek something to be passionate about, they want love, a great relationship, but they heard their father, or mother, repeat a thousand times that money is more important, and as they were children, they were very vulnerable to the words of their parents. So as adults, there are many battles inside of them, just on that topic alone, which become responsible for **creating dissociations between the desires of their hearts, and the dysfunctional programming they have not yet managed to escape from**. This can have so much impact in a person's life, from their choices of careers, their goals, what they derive pleasure from... Those battles wear us down, keep us away from the present, parts of you running one way, and parts of you running in the opposite direction, or standing still waiting for the storms to pass.

That is why it can become very hard to move in one firm direction, to your dreams, to your best life, as all your parts have their own agendas when burdened by the past, running from all kinds of things, and also running away from life. In the prior situation, a practice to heal could be writing out by hand, a hundred, or a thousand times "money is not the most important factor in my life, love is", and holding a loving intent for your future, to release yourself from that programming. You can do this for anything you would like, as part of healing and reprogramming yourself to a better state, a more loving capacity. This can help to bring back many of those parts stuck in dysfunctional programming, in pain, to bring them back to order, to feel and think in unison, vibrating your being towards one defined goal.

And you can do this for all of your life, all those things you think have emotional energy hung up in the past with, and also for the good, to practice expanding your gratitude. To visualize everything, to imagine a better outcome, to create it in your mind like a movie with a better ending, or write it out, talk about it with a friend, or a therapist. And revisit the good stuff too, take the time in your mind (or in person) to tell the people that have positively affected your life, your journey, thank them for it, explain how your life got better for your interactions with them, what they might have done that you are grateful for, and remember the positive impact of great experiences, how they have helped to mold you into a better person.

Again, I know I focus more on the stuff we need to heal from, to let go of, **but don't neglect the good in your life**, and in your past. Gratitude is so important, it is like rocket fuel that feeds love, to take you where your dreams might lead you.

Positive reinforcement, we all know how important it is, yet we so often neglect to practice it on us.

The need to feel some pain: To heal, we need to feel the pain of what we experienced, and love and gratitude can help to pull us back out of the darkness when we've had the courage to face what was in it. But many people are under the impression that to feel pain, is like a punishment, maybe because it often relates to their childhood, of being punished, and how emotionally upsetting it was. But as an adult, to heal, we must go through it, even to face many of our present situations there's often emotional suffering we must endure, from defeat, setbacks, losses, relationships going sour. So if we maintain the habit of running away from emotional pain, then we'll end up accumulating much more of it. It is not punishment to go through the pains of the past, just like someone going through chemotherapy to cure their cancer. The pain is not punishment, it is necessary to kill something "bad" inside of them that is growing, and might kill them. Emotional baggage does cause various forms of illnesses and diseases, not just emotional suffering, and in a way, it does kill us little by little, so the pain to go through it, to heal, can be seen as chemotherapy to cancer, it has a greater purpose, and the more we succeed, to more alive we get. But we must do it with care and understanding, otherwise we risk falling into the pain and just wallow in it, then it serves no purpose.

A small example for seeing the past as it was: As a child, you came home from school one day and tried to share a story about how your teacher was mean to you, dismissive of your need for help for an exercise. Your mother had just got back from her work, and had a tough day. She dismisses your need to talk about the pain you experienced at school, pain that was quite real for you, but you then find yourself obligated to suppress it. Usually your mother is there for you, but she gives herself the "right" to dismiss your request this time, rationalizing that most of the time she is quite attentive to your needs. Children don't rationalize very well, in fact, almost every time their needs are not met, it can register just the same as abuse, and can result in trauma, meaning that the pain stays around long after the situation has been experienced. In this example, a typically supportive mother, with a few lacks now and then. That child might become a fairly well adjusted adult, who has a great fondness for his/her mother. But, there is still a lot of unprocessed stuff in the background, that might remain unprocessed. For to process that trauma, the person would need to revisit his/her past in a different light, a different perspective, one that "dares" to look upon their mother as imperfect, that dares to blame, that dares to ventilate out the pains of the past **for how they felt in the moment**, and the trauma that resulted. Again, self-reflection, different perspective, and improved E-Glasses to see things as they are, past the "respect" we feel we need to maintain, past the need to see our parents as perfect, and allowing ourselves to see the "good, the bad and the ugly", just as they are, without embellishments, or suppression.

That is not an easy thing to do, especially when we truly had "loving/mostly loving" parents. But to truly process the pain, we have to accept all there is involved within that pain, no matter where it comes from, what created it, and why. To understand the imperfections of people, to understand that as children, we were needy in regards to our emotions, we didn't rationalize much, nor understood well the difficulties parents face and how challenging it might be to raise children while managing their own stuff. As adults, we often dismiss our childhood pain for the same reasons. But as children, the pain was quite real, and the repercussions, the trauma, is also quite real, and still there, dormant or not, because we have repressed and ignored most of it. I will go deeper in the parent/child relationship later, and how much it contributes to our trauma without us knowing, especially in "good enough" parenting situations. This was to give an example of the types of abuse that we generally don't consider as abuse, but nonetheless results in trauma.

Abuse is often not even Felt, or Dismissed as Something to just "get over"

I focus on abuse in this section, and anything that results in repressed emotions and dysfunctional conditioning as that is a great part of what is required for us to do in our **"Life Review"**, to free everything in our being that is stuck there, the imperfections keeping parts of us separated from the whole.

Think of a Muay Thai fighter who has conditioned his shins to become insensitive to pain. Yet when he fights, even though he might not feel the pain from his blows, the skin will still show signs of trauma, cuts and bruises, same goes for our emotions. The trauma sets in, even if we don't feel the pain of it because our past trauma has made us insensitive to some levels of pain, from low to high levels, matching our trauma. People that have experienced high levels of trauma can become insensitive to low and medium levels of it, but the effects will still be there. Like a woman being violently abused in childhood, now tolerates being violently abused by her spouse, or thinking that medium levels of abuse are "okay", until she can heal from it, and see it for what it is. Many people actually seek out abuse, from others, or themselves, because they have become insensitive to everything else. Like people with addictions, drugs, hurting themselves in various ways, or allowing people to hurt them. This happens much more than we realize, many people suffer on a daily basis, yet most of it goes unnoticed. I understand why to a certain extent it can be depressing to think of all of it, but as long as we ignore it, nothing will ever change. So, like the band-aid, if we collectively agree to go through our pain, to "exorcise" it, then maybe we will collectively suffer more for a few decades, but after, if we do it right and don't give up, wow, I am convinced the results would be breathtaking, and love would be available for all.

Okay, I know, in the last section I talked about the next sections as being "brighter", and here I am talking about abuse and trauma. But, see, there *is* a rainbow at the end of it, and giving hope that we can do something about it, not just suffer the narcissism in our world and all the pain from that...

> *"True emotional healing doesn't happen without feeling. The only way out is through..."* – **Jessica Moore**

So, something that creates a painful response *is* abuse, and should not be dismissed, even if we think it "should" not be abusive, or even if we don't feel it in the moment. Like in adult relationships, often sensitive people get hurt by insensitive people, then when the sensitive people respond to the pain, the insensitive people dismiss it, saying stuff like "you are being too sensitive", "get over it", or even "If you don't stop whining, I'll give you something to cry about", many a father's favorite "go to" as an alternative to shut the hell up. Those are typical responses by narcissists or people with low E.Q./E.M.. Since they can't feel most of the pain in their own beings, they think that others do not, or should not either. Often it is because they have experienced pain in childhood, and their response was to "toughen up", to dismiss the pain, or repress it so deep they lost their connections to most of their feelings. Then as adults, they simply don't feel or understand emotional pain any longer, not even the emotional pain that comes from physical abuse, and think others should be the same. But if/when they finally figure out something is wrong in their lives, and they seek to start feeling again, only the strongest emotions and feelings will do, such as violent anger and addictive behaviors, until they find a way to heal from those long forgotten experiences.

If you feel pain, then it is abusive to you. And maybe you have become overly sensitive to stuff that most people are not, and that's okay, accept that. Your feelings are your own, don't allow people to dismiss them. If you find that you are overly sensitive, then the more you heal your wounds, the more your sensitivity will come closer to normal. But in the process, accept that you are overly sensitive for a while. Now, getting stuck in overly sensitive mode can be a drag, so to accept that of yourself, be careful to not cast it out all around you. A healing journey is taken in progressive steps, staying overly sensitive is not an option to really heal, it shows you are not progressing. If it lasts, change what you are doing, or seek better help.

We have all become insensitive to a certain degree, and our sensitivities have become mixed up also, we often don't "feel" the right things at the right time. Like many people have issues with money for instance, they always feel they will run out of it, afraid of being poor, even if their bank accounts are overflowing with it. That is an example of trauma that has been mixed up with various complicated things over the years, and the person can't see reality for what it is anymore, in relationship to money in this example. They carry the fear of being poor, even if their bank account screams out the opposite in large bold font on their statements. We do that so often, for so many things. And the more mixed up our feeling system gets, the more we are prone to experiencing further abuse and trauma without even realizing it, which is quite unfortunate. Often our unhealed pain actually increases our chances of experiencing more pain that will further go unhealed, adding to our emotional burden. That is part of the reason why it can seem like we take 2 steps back for every 3 steps we move forward. Untangling the complicated webs of our emotional trauma takes time and dedication. So, finding out how much you are willing to invest in your own self, your own love, is part of what will determine the quality and depth of the relationship you develop with yourself.

How far are you willing to go to prove your love for those things inside of you that have been suppressed for so long? Would you be like those soldiers that risk their lives, that risk getting lost themselves, tortured, imprisoned, to rescue a few POW's in some distant country? Are you willing to go that far within you, through all your fears, to reconsider all of your relationships, all of your earlier experiences, to rescue those lost/dissociated parts?

Trauma is real for all of us, its impact can be seen all over the world; in every abuse, in every conflict, in terrorism, in greed, in jealousy, in dictatorships, in excessive consumption, in addictions, in sexual exploitation... No truly loving being would engage in any of those behaviors, and when we look at the world, it can sometimes be hard to see anything but trauma being manifested out in people's actions, but there is hope yet to be found.

The Wounds of Yesterday Haunt the Times of Today, and of Tomorrow

To put things in perspective:

Editorial Review: *"The trauma caused by childhood neglect, sexual or domestic abuse and war wreaks havoc in our bodies, says Bessel van der Kolk in The Body Keeps the Score. Van der Kolk draws on 30 years of experience to argue powerfully that trauma is one of the West's most urgent public health issues. Packed with science and human stories, the book is an intense read, the struggle and resilience of his patients is very moving."* – **Shaoni Bhattacharya**, New Scientist

This an editorial review for *"**The Body Keeps the Score: Brain, Mind, and Body in the Healing of Trauma**"*, a #1 *New York Times* best selling book on healing from trauma, I recommend it to anyone that is serious about getting a fresh start on life. It is a bit technical/clinical, but still a good read even for an average "non-professional" person.

A short excerpt from the book: *"Over the years our research has repeatedly found that chronic emotional abuse and neglect can be just as devastating as physical abuse and sexual molestation."*

The author of the book, *Bessel van der Kolk*, as of this writing is a psychiatrist with decades of clinical experience in dealing with trauma, he is also a professor, and founder and medical director of the Trauma Center in Brookline, Massachusetts. He knows what he is talking about, and is firm in his opinions of just how much our trauma influences so much of our current lives, and how it is much more widespread than we realize.

Another partial review: *"In this compelling book we learn that as our minds desperately try to leave trauma behind, our bodies keep us trapped in the past with wordless emotions and feelings. These inner disconnections cascade into ruptures in social relationships with disastrous effects on marriages, families, and friendships."* – **Stephen W. Porges, Ph.D**

A lot of what I discuss in this book is about that, a mind/body "whole" approach to healing, understanding that we all have trauma even if a lot of people don't think so, to not feel bad about it, it is a fact of life, and how important it is for people to do more to heal from it.

Life can get busy, and we can get lost dealing with details that seem very important to us in the moment, but in the long run, those details end up sucking too much of our lives into them, and our inner selves stay/get lost somewhere along the way. Those that would insist on saying to not "dwell on the past" are quite ignorant of just how much our past affects our present, and our future. Our history is replete of true teachers, gurus and philosophers that have said time and time again that the best life can only be had with self-reflection, but how many great people have said that you should simply forget the past?

The Quest for Love

Everything we do in life comes from our desire to love, and be loved, so we can postulate that everything that people do that is hurtful, is simply a desire for love gone wrong.

Even murderers and rapists, their deepest desire is for love, but because they have been hurt in so many ways, the search, and expression, of love gets so distorted by all sorts of pains and wounds inside of them, that it becomes a very unhealthy manifestation of all sorts of things that become so far removed from love. Thinking again of those E-Glasses, all twisted and broken, how can anyone find what they are truly looking for in life with them? Like searching for a treasure when our map is heavily stained and full of holes. How can anyone express their heart's desires when all of that energy gets twisted and contorted in so many ways? This can explain why a woman who was abused in childhood finds herself an abusive partner. Her E-Glasses have mixed up abusive people with love, and that is all she can see. Not that she doesn't want love, she simply cannot see, or feel it, for what it is, or know how to find it. We do that over and over again, we all want the same kind of things out of life, but our E-Glasses often keeps us going around in circles, not seeing the forest for the trees, or the trees for the forest.

"Most of the evil in this world is done by people with good intentions..." – **T.S. Eliot**

"Good intentions" can come out very bad when they have to go through a lot of our repressed stuff, our ego, and conditioning. People often act in very selfish and hurtful ways without even knowing it. And when people get hurt by these *seemingly good intentions gone bad*, the ones that "tried" to act in good ways are often hurt themselves, as they only see the good intentions, and don't understand how their "good intentions" could have caused pain to the other, as they simply cannot process that kind of information unless they heal.

So, this "haunting", is of all the things in your current life that are not what you would have chosen had you known yourself at a deeper level, had you known enough about yourself to heal all the trauma, all the conditioning of your past, and had not been influenced by the desires and goals, or abuse, of various people and factors in your environment. And again, by haunting, is that we often don't see it, we don't realize it. Like unseen and unheard ghosts of the past making us decide all sorts of things that are not very well suited for us, yet can "appear" to be good enough. So many people spend so much of their time wishing that their present moment was different than what it is. That is not a way to live a great life, it is a clear indication that something needs to change.

> *"Sometimes we must undergo hardships, breakups, and narcissistic wounds, which shatter the flattering image that we had of ourselves, in order to discover two truths: that we are not who we thought we were; and that the loss of a cherished pleasure is not necessarily the loss of true happiness and well-being..."* — **Jean-Yves Leloup**

Again, arm yourself with as much knowledge as you can, but still be kind. It can get frustrating, sometimes you move forward, sometimes you move back, but don't give up, you are worth the fight!

MUSICAL INTERLUDE: Speaking of not giving up, for the journey and where it takes us, give this one a listening to: ***Never Give Up***, by **Sia** (Pretty cool video as well, part of the soundtrack from the movie *Lion*)

So yes, it does Always go back to our Childhood, well, often Enough

The famous Freudian thing, about our mother and father, as the sources of many of our struggles...

That is why self-reflection, and reviewing your whole life, becomes so important, and of course, to look at things the way they were, all of it. Therapists often focus on those early years as they know just how much of our current lives can be affected by those experiences, even the ones before our memories, as most people can only remember from the ages of 4 or 5 and on. A lot of stuff happens before then, and maybe self-reflection might not bring back the actual memories, but you can still touch upon the feelings, and learn to break free from their ill effects.

"All children should be taught to unconditionally accept, approve, admire, appreciate, forgive, trust, and ultimately, love their own person..." – **Asa Don Brown**

Unfortunately every parent falls short of doing this to a high enough degree as to cause no trauma, no wounds at all to their children. So if someone reading this thinks they don't have enough trauma to bother even trying, then they are living an illusion. Yes, some people have pretty good lives, but we are far short of having a plenitude of true leaders in our world today. And if many of the people that are already *well enough* decide to become even better, then maybe they can be our next "great" leaders, to start those great enterprises and projects of tomorrow that will take us to new levels of living in our society. And maybe even becoming the leaders of future colonies on other planets, as I don't think we should consider doing that until we figure ourselves out on Earth first, otherwise we will only be exporting the same old stuff that we struggle here with.

*Another great book on this topic you might want to check out: *Adult Children of Emotionally Immature Parents: How to Heal from Distant, Rejecting, or Self-Involved Parents*, by **Lindsay C. Gibson.**

You need to develop the proper skills and understanding to heal all of those parts left in childhood, to become the "mother and father" that your inner child ache for. That is the process of "re-parenting" yourself that everyone needs to undertake. It is part of the spiritual journey, to emotionally and psychologically separate from your parents, to become an emotionally mature adult, to stand on your own "two legs". Which is necessary to increase your level of E.M. beyond merely acceptable or functional, to higher levels where dreams become possible.

I have used the terms "Re-Parenting" and "Inner-Child" here, and those that wish to learn more about them, again, you can find many books and other resources on these topics. They are worth checking into, but I will limit their use to save some space for other things.

But again, the line between processing, letting go, healing, and the idea of blaming can be difficult to navigate. Who can we blame really? Knowing that trauma and abuse are often passed down from one generation to another, then who do you blame? Your parents, or their parents for abusing them, or theirs... **Hundreds of years, thousands of years, abuse, violence, passed on from one generation to the next**, and once you have experienced that abuse, it is difficult not to pass it down to others. To stop the cycles, to break the patterns, is to heal the whole timeline, is to remove all of that pain from humanity. So maybe we will need to think of something, to put a plan in motion, and maybe big sacrifices will need to be made for several generations, to stop the spread of all of those ills to future generations once and for all.

Maybe what we really need, what our world is desperate for, is a good shaking, instead of being gently stirred to death...

Sometimes we just need to accept what has happened to us, even if we don't want to, to go through those darkened forests, just as when children, the need to grow, to mature, and to gain the courage to look under our bed before getting into it, or in the closet, or to sleep without the light. As adults, we need to do the same, but within ourselves.

Yes, emotional and psychological healing can be tricky, and I have mentioned many times already that we do not have all the answers, so I do talk about various systems for your benefit, for you to be able to find something that works best for your situation and learning abilities. None of them are perfect, some are more clinical, others more spiritual, depending on your beliefs and strategies, you might get much more from one or the other, the important thing is to try and make progress. Living with emotional baggage is not fun, I know it very well, and it hurts us in more ways than we would care to really understand sometimes, but left untouched, it will cause much more pain to you in the long run.

In his book *"The Emotion Code"*, Dr. Bradley Nelson calls trapped emotions **The Invisible Epidemic.** Which gives you a good idea of what professionals are now coming to understand about how our stuck emotions can wreak havoc not only in our own personal lives, but in the world at large.

When we are very "unhealed", a lot of things don't even have a chance to come to our active thinking process, so you don't even know what you are missing out on, you don't even have a chance to think about them, to contemplate, to choose. So your options can be extremely limited to only things that can run the gauntlet of your fears, repressed stuff, trauma, to make it into your mind for you to even be aware of those things. We can think that we have choices, **but when those choices don't even "come to mind"**, then you become very limited. Like the idea of working in a different city, your fears might completely block that option from becoming an active thought, so you might not check out any job postings anywhere else, yet your heart might be aching for such a change. And this applies to so many other things, like being brought up to think women should just get married and have children, simple as that, and unless you confront where that conditioning comes from, to not accept it, then you will always fight against it. Maybe deep down, you do want children, but the conditioning might make you resent having them if you do, because the decision was not yours, even if you chose the same thing. Or not having children, because you fought the conditioning head on, instead of freeing yourself from it, and end up being resentful. If your conditioning calls the shots, then your life will never be stellar, to not fully accept how it is, even if you would make similar choices from your own deeper self.

Our "Dysfunctional Emotional Matrix"

Consider these next few sections as a bit, experimental, things I am working on that I think can be of value to share... So I am not saying that this is our true reality, but, it makes sense and can be useful to understand the important topics a bit better.

The ideas of Emotional Maturity, and what can prevent us from it, our broken E-Glasses, trauma, our various blocked energy systems, the Ego and who we think this "I" person is within us... Even dreams, we all dream, many believe they offer important insights into our lives, into who we are, to help us heal, to connect to those deeper parts of us, but we understand very little of them still. So yes, it can all be tremendously complicated. Humans have been trying to figure themselves out for so long, through psychology, philosophy, dreams, Gods, beliefs, culture, and even macrame...

Just "we/I", we are not even sure what that means, what is it, this "us" we refer to ourselves as? Consciousness, our reality, our life, when we behave in one way at work, then another way at home, how do we do that? Do we have a "work" template that we put on, like a suit, then take it off after work, or are there more than one of us taking on different roles as we see fit? I actually believe that we all have multiple personalities, the only difference with the people that have the actual "disorder" is that they completely assume individual personalities, as opposed to us (those that don't have it that is, I shouldn't assume who is reading this), we have a unifying controller that stays at the helm. Like for the orchestra idea, the conductor, we all have one within us, people with multiple personality disorder completely assume the role of a violinist at times, or a member of the choral, others that don't have it, are always the conductor, but they still have all the members of the orchestra inside of them.

Consider this quote:

"The greatest sources of our suffering are the lies we tell ourselves..." – **Elvin V. Semrad**

Who are these "we" and "ourselves" that he refers to? How can one part of us tell a lie to another part of us? How can lies even exist within us in the first place? Should we not know everything about us if we are just "one" person? How can one part hide things from another part on purpose? And this man worked in a psychiatric ward as a psychiatrist (and professor) for many a moon and not only became famous, but very good at what he did, he should know a few things about personalities and consciousness.

I'll leave the question of *us* aside for a bit of time.

Now, what on Earth am I getting into, ***Dysfunctional Emotional Matrix***, after this existential "who am I" stuff?

Well, think about our Emotional Matrix as a second brain in a way, not an actual "brain", but a similar complicated network of connections, energies, information, **but for our emotions and feelings** instead of data and thoughts.

*Some experts are now considering our gut as our second brain, and seeing that the vagus nerve is an almost one way traffic of information to the brain from the gut, up to 90% of it, and the collective of bacteria in our gut far outweighs those of the rest of our body, so who is running the show?

So, without defining it *exactly*, think about the *Emotional Matrix* as some kind of neural net/system that includes all of our emotional experiences, everything. And just as the dysfunctions of the mind/brain create a secondary system/self we call the **Ego**, the secondary system created out of the dysfunctions of the Emotional Matrix (trauma, fears and such), I call the **Ega**, which some refer to as the *pain body* (Aha, and the plot thickens!). And we could also call the Ego the "pain mind", or, yes, some of you got it: Dysfunctional **Mind** Matrix!

To recap, as some of you might be screaming out "what the!?". So, the Ego, the pain mind, and the Dysfunctional Mind Matrix/D.M.M., **all** the same, just different ways of referring to them. Same as with the Ega, the pain body, and the Dysfunctional Emotional Matrix/D.E.M., **all** the same as well.

So our Dysfunctional Emotional Matrix gets layered over reality, warping our relationship with it, with others, taints what we see and feel, layers of our past, layers of our trauma, layers of conditioning and unhealthy programming, all pulling us further away from the truth of the moment, from other people, and ourselves... Divisions upon divisions, separations, keeping us apart, making so many people around us as enemies, competitors, people to be afraid of, to avoid, or to yearn for... In a way, it keeps us living a thousand lies, over and over again, lies that get projected onto everything we see, feel, touch, experience. One dysfunctional filter over the other, pulling us further away from love, from our deeper selves, that is how people can become human traffickers, murderers, dictators... All those separations combine to create a false self/reality that becomes the antithesis to love.

I did say this was experimental, a sort of mind exercise meant to see things in a different way, observing our selves in compartmentalized ways to understand how the whole is held together and interacts with itself.

Our Dissociated Selves

Doesn't it make sense, that when we experience certain emotions and feelings that we can't process for whatever reason, like one of our parents hitting us, we have a part, or parts of us believing they should love us (which is quite normal), and then other parts witness/experience something that is far from love. So those parts become in conflict as their reality is so different, and anything in conflict within our system **cannot remain in our consciousness**, as our consciousness is whole, nothing can exist within it **if it is not in union with itself**. No separation can remain in our consciousness, in the present moment as "one". So anything that is not whole, that has conflicted elements, gets moved into the subconscious until it can be properly processed at some point. Those things that are in conflict always have a mind and emotion component (**Ego and Ega**), as the thought and the feeling of the moment don't match, which happens often in childhood.

The subconscious then becomes part of our dreams, and nightmares. So the **us** that is part of our consciousness when we are awake, then moves into that realm made up of our dissociated parts when we sleep. Our nightmares are the worst of them, our worst pains, our worst sufferings. There is more to our dreams than this, but that's part of it. **And unfortunately, the things we run away from in our nightmares is often us**, us and the pains responsible for keeping that *us* lost in our subconscious.

Let's say you had a horrible parent, who at times burned your skin with lit matches, yes, that kind of horrible. That trauma can become a nightmare, which you run away from. But, the terror you are running away from is your own self, the one that is still crying the pain of being burnt, and all it wants is your attention, to help soothe it, so it runs after you in your dreams, but you run away from it. So you need to face the pain that was caused, and also the source that caused it. To build a relationship with yourself, you need to build a relationship between your dissociated parts, so that they stop being separated from you, and reclaimed as part of your present self. I'm not saying all nightmares get created that way, but many do, and also why it is so important to face our internal suffering, and why it is there.

For the technical people out there, pay attention to this: Ha, as if that could *actually* be done, to give some money in exchange for a greater capacity to be present and focused, who comes up with these expressions? And what does it mean really, to "pay" attention? Bygones... Okay, think about a computer and buffers, memory systems and all of that... When we give it too much to work on, whatever the operating system cannot handle at any moment in time, it puts in a buffer to deal with later. Lets say this "buffer" is like our **D.E.M**. and **D.M.M.**, Ega and Ego, anything our system could not deal with at the time it happened (like abuse and violence, fears...), it stores it somewhere for later processing, if it ever does get processed. Except for us, this *somewhere* keeps pulling our attention, our awareness, our "I" right into it, **to such an extent that we believe that it is our true home**, we settle in and pull out the Lazy Boy (or the torture rack), and watch all of what is going on through illusory glasses, like a big television screen instead of living our own life in the present, and it f**ks us up big time. (Not sure about rating systems in books, so just ** to be on the safe side...)

IMPORTANT NOTE: All kinds of things accumulate in those buffers, that become part of our Dysfunctional Emotional Matrix, not just the idea of trauma. Even having a co-worker borrowing a pen, and not returning it, irking you but you not saying anything about it, someone cutting through the line at the grocery store, and no one mentions it, as if "letting it go", but obviously a bit annoying, and your system does not let go of it. **All emotions and feelings that are not expressed, reconciled, big and small, *must* be processed by your system and integrated as a whole, stored for later processing, or discarded.** When we fully process things as they happen, then the experience becomes part of you (or gets let go of), without emotional attachments, so they are whole, not fractured. If you borrow some money, even a few dollars, and don't give it back, or say something mean and not apologize, all those little things, once your system interacts with something, once it sees, experiences, hears, smells, touches, **your system must make sense of those experiences**. Your active mind can dismiss something as not so important (like someone not returning a pen), but your system as a whole does not have that luxury, it must process things as they are, it cannot just rethink it into something else, it does not forget, and it does not re-manufacture reality to suit its needs. They all accumulate in your system until you process them properly. And those accumulated things all contribute to a lesser life in many different ways, another way of considering trauma.

You can choose to "move on", *but your system cannot*, it must do something with everything it experiences, **it always keeps the score as long as there is a score to keep.**

It can feel a bit dispiriting to think about it all, and to think of all those past things to go through, so it is important to try much harder in the present at least to not just let things slip away into those buffers. When you feel something, see something, say it out loud, express, discuss, make sure you are okay with it, that the situation has a proper ending, maybe not perfect, maybe not to your advantage, but at least it should *feel* right to you. And if you can't find a proper solution that feels right to you in the moment, say you'll have to think about it, just don't leave it unresolved. Yes, a non-returned pen can contribute to your trauma if you are not truly okay with it, contributing to issues in your system that you must fight against, even if small, and even if you eventually forget it, all those things lowers your emotional intelligence and maturity. So often nowadays in our society we are encouraged to forget "the small stuff", like people cutting in line, or sarcasm, turning a blind eye to many things. All contributing to decreasing our overall level of E.M., becoming less compassionate and less present, and loving ourselves less in the process. To dismiss things that should not be dismissed does not make us more compassionate, even if on the surface it can appear that way, it makes us more dispassionate and uncaring, and distances ourselves from others, and us.

"The only thing necessary for the triumph of evil is for good men (*and women) to do nothing (*or say nothing)..."
– Edmund Burke

I allowed myself a bit of creativity with that one, besides, it is not a direct quote, more an attribution based on a longer letter, and, it is not truly clear where those sentiments really originated from...

Well, this turned out to be longer than anticipated...

So, without self-reflection, first, we will have such a hard time processing all the stuff that got stored in our buffers, the Ego and Ega, the dysfunctional pain matrices... And also, we won't ever get to realize the extent of how much our lives are spent living outside of the present moment, and instead living in the "Matrix", that is our ***pain body*** and ***pain mind* combined**, they become an integrated whole, a second and illusory "reality".

"Unfortunately there can be no doubt that man is, on the whole, less good than he imagines himself or wants to be. Everyone carries a shadow, and the less it is embodied in the individual's conscious life, the blacker and denser it is. At all

counts, it forms an unconscious snag, thwarting our most well-meant intentions..." – **Carl Jung**

Again, why oh why am I getting into this, really?

Because it is all very relevant, and I believe all of that is part of what we will need to focus on in the decades to come if we want to up the game in our healing process. To reverse the tides of psychological illnesses like depression and ADHD and anti-social behaviors (including narcissism), as they are all increasing at an alarming rate. Drugs are not the solution, healing is. We need to re-invent the tools we use to help people to heal and overcome the difficulties this new fast-paced, and very materialistic world, are creating for us, emotionally and psychologically speaking. I'm not saying that I have all the answers we're looking for, but I do believe I am at least looking in the right direction, and others should add their knowledge to help guide us to a better place.

The "whole being" approach, not only body, not only mind, not just thoughts, or just feelings and emotions. All, including past and present, and future, they all go together, as deep down, we are all experiencing everything at the same time. Time breaks down deep within us, which is why healing can be so complicated. When a situation triggers a past trauma, we experience the repressed trauma/experience as if it was today, **because for that part of us, that past *is* today**. So you can think of these D.E.M. and D.M.M. as energy matrices that are not anchored in the present, they are all in flux, past, future, back and forth... And the more we heal them, the more present we get, as they are the ones pulling us into the past and future, into trauma, into wounds, into unfulfilled desires and all sorts of unreconciled experiences we have had.

Just like in the movie *The Matrix*, at first, Neo is living in an illusion, a "Matrix", until he takes the red pill, which is meant to break his illusions. Parts of us are also living in a Matrix of our own, one of the mind, and one of the body, thoughts and emotions. Those parts that are not present, in pain, in fears, living in the past, in the future, in regrets, in shame, all accumulate in our Dysfunctional Matrices, and help to create a world of illusions within us. To develop our E-Glasses, **is to develop the capacity to see those illusions for what they are.** To see how the abuse of our current partner is a replay of the abuse from our father or mother, to see how we keep freaking out when someone calls us stupid because we now remember that our older sibling kept doing that to us when we were young. Then we can do what is necessary to heal, to take the red pill, over and over, and little by little, those parts of us lost in our "Matrices" will now come and join us in the reality of the present. It is not a "one shot deal" like in the movie unfortunately, and it will never be completely over, as no perfection can exist. But at least we can aim for "perfect enough" to have a great life, as "perfect" is not necessary. And, always be mindful of those that would try to make you swallow blue pills, the ones that would feed you lies, that would seek to make you angry, to keep you in misery, that would try to compel you to cheat, to engage in drama and such, those dreaded gaslighters. Learn to distinguish people's intent, as what you allow from them, to accept their ill gifts will lead you away from emotional maturity, back into illusions. Red pills lead us to life, and blue pills, to death. Learn how to identify, and say no, to those coming to you with blue pills, no thanks, sayonara!

"By healing the parts of ourselves that are frozen in the past, we are able to bring them back into the present – And each time we do this we become less fragmented, and more whole..." – **Jessica Moore**

So, to not go back into our past with our special E-Glasses, is to keep accepting the false views of it, and the lies we tell ourselves to cover it all up... To not see this "Dysfunctional Matrix" for what it is, and how it creates a false self, like the

Ego and Ega, is to accept a lesser life. And understand that the Ego strives to have a life of its own, as if it believes it is its own creation. Your ego will do everything to remain in charge, and keep you as its own star attraction, **because without you, it is nothing, and it knows that on a certain level**. So the ego becomes conscious of itself on some level, and seeks to live. Narcissists are people that are obviously living in a world of their own, and in a way, that's exactly what happens, their own private, personal Matrix that they carry around wherever they go. They *become* their ego, and also how they become so anti-social, as they are removed from society while in their Matrix. The real world isn't there for them, their illusions become their reality, and reality, an illusion.

Well, seems like I did it again, I try to keep it simple, but off I go, hope you are keeping up...

The Selfish Ego and the Illusions we Fight Against

"The ego, however, is not who you really are. The ego is your self-image, it is your social mask, it is the role you are playing. Your social mask thrives on approval. It wants control, and it is sustained by power because it lives in fear..."
– Ram Dass

Again, the term "Ego" has been known for many years, I am just rethinking it as a system comprising of an accumulation of our experiences we have not reconciled, not processed, a system that our awareness gets caught up in. So, the bigger our Ego, the more our awareness gets sucked into it, the more selfish we become, and the more we function like a computer, or robot, all dysfunctional conditioning and programming, devoid of love or compassion. The more we act as if we are the only individuals alive, the only individuals deserving of all the riches, all the attention, as if the world revolves around us, like we were the best gift to humanity.

The matrix is within us, and we need to find a way of pulling ourselves out of it, little by little, by dissolving/healing the components that keep it operational.

"Love is happy when it is able to give something. The ego is happy when it is able to take something..." – **Osho**

Love is the one force that unites us all, in compassion and empathy, in the present moment. That is why people who have a lot of unhealed trauma and conditioning are frequently lonely and depressed, they are mostly not even living in life, in the present moment, they are indeed mostly alone in their individual matrices. No matter what they do, unless they reduce the size of their Ego and Ega, they will not be able to assuage that terrible feeling of loneliness that their lives have become. That is why they often resort to drugs and addictions. Sex, companionship, friends, all cannot help them, healing is the only thing that will work for the long term. A person can avoid their pain for a while, but as long as it remains, it will always be a threat to their greater existence.

So yes, in the end, love *is* the answer, it is what the red pill is made out of, in this book anyway... But to get there, there are many roads we must understand, to let go of many things, to grow our capacity for love. Love itself is free, but it can only be held by those who have managed to master themselves at a high enough degree, and understand what that really means.

GO FOR A WALK: Now might be a good time to take a bit of a break to let things soak in. Walking while contemplating is a great exercise to let your mind wander, to let your being do what it needs to do to reconcile the thoughts of your mind, and the feelings in your heart. Your system does this when you sleep, but it often gets overloaded. Plus, while sleeping, without your conscious awareness present, your "being" sometimes needs to make decisions on its own, without "your" input. I know it sounds kind of weird to think about it this way, your being making decisions without you being present, but that happens when you sleep (unless you dream actively/knowingly). But only with the small stuff, the rest will need your attention, otherwise it gets stored away to be processed later, and a lot of things accumulate because of it, of our incapacity to make proper decisions when they happen.

If nature is close, go there, walk amongst the trees, the water, in a park, along a river, great for reflecting within yourself, and to process things so they don't end up being caught in your buffers, or to reflect on the things already there.

Rewriting the Past, but Understanding it First

What goes in, must come out, what gets lost, must be found, what is mixed, must get matched...

So, healing is in effect reconciling the Ego and Ega. The more we do that, the smaller they get, the more our pain dissolves, and the more of the true *us* gets revealed, or becomes. Maybe that is what that is, our subconscious getting smaller, less dark things in our inner closets, so we live more in our conscious mind, more of *us* to be present *with*. And the more we do that, the more the effects of our past in our every day lives is lessened.

> *"The more one judges, the less one loves..."*
> **– Honoré de Balzac**

Again, taking the red pill, is to do what we can to see the world for what it is, and ourselves too, and that means healing our D.E.M./D.M.M.. Getting over our Ego and Ega, and using those E-Glasses to see much clearer, behind the curtain, through the programming, beyond the lies and deceit, all of it... With greater emotional maturity and clarity, all of your new experiences are not only easier to get through, but they also get integrated into your system much more efficiently, in a healthier manner, and what you don't need, you discard right away.

But, that red pill can be quite bitter (which is why many people avoid it), and you'll need to repeat the experience of it many many times. Think about it as horrible tasting cold syrup, you hate the taste of it, but you take it to feel better, your health depends on going beyond the temporary displeasure. For every one of those red pills you are willing to swallow, and willing to do what it requires of you to let go, such as maybe forgiving, apologizing, being angry for a while, changing jobs, letting go of a relationship, your life will improve. So each red pill that you have the courage to take will each demand something different of you, and you must comply to its demands, otherwise the pill will have no effect. Like the purifying fires of love, it burns anything that isn't made of the same quality, of truth, of empathy, it can hurt, but in the end, you'll be much better for the experience.

So yes, re-writing the past, it can be done!

Really, well, maybe not *re-writing* the actual past, the material/physical nature of it, but that's not important anyway, so why bother? I'm talking about the "real" past, and what could be the real past? Anything that our system got hooked up with, gets conditioned by, and still holds; emotions, feelings, perceptions, beliefs, what else is there anyway?

We live our lives based on how we feel, how we interact with the present, our beliefs, the effects we have on other people, the sum of all thoughts and desires. They all blend into one another in a giant soup of energy we call the present moment. Matter comes and goes, **but the impact, the effect, of who we are as we change from one moment to the other, that remains.** And that is what we can change of the past, how it changed us, our relationship to it, and to others within it as well.

Your relationship to what has happened to you is what matters most, change that relationship, and you change how those things affect you in the present moment, that is how you change your reality.

And doesn't it all make sense with the "increasing our emotional maturity" thing, having a better life, better relationships, love and all of that? Maybe not in a *Rosetta Stone* kind of way, but still, decent so far I think.

Why do you keep settling for less, why do you keep doing things that are not moving you towards a better destination? Year after year, why do you think that is? Do you think it is because you just can't do anything more? Or maybe there is something inside of you that keeps making you miss the boat, for the life of you, you can't figure it out, but time passes, and nothing changes.

We can do better, you can do better, I know you can, we all just need a bit of motivation, the proper incentives, and a better understanding of who we are, and where we want to go!

It's all Coming Back!

Our Ego will fight back against anything that will try to take power away from it. You can witness this in the world, those with huge Egos will fight tooth and nail against anyone who would challenge them, their authority, their power, their "rightfulness", our inner Ego does the same thing. Which makes healing more complicated, which is why it is important to understand how it works, and be able to circumvent its defenses.

I am repeating these few things again as we are nearing the middle of the book, as I want to make certain they are understood enough before we start the second part, in which I have a bunch of new things that I want to repeat over and over;)

> *"Anything you avoid in life will come back, over and over again, until you're willing to face it—to look deeply into its true nature..."* – **Adyashanti**

That is why love, compassion, empathy, vulnerability, are some of your most important tools to free those repressed and suppressed things that cause you so much harm in life, and will be some of the main topics in the next sections, which will make it a bit lighter and more encouraging, to help raise the bar on **Hope**. With those tools, you can use them to look at the things that we tend to avoid looking at, those things that make us not want to open our inner doors, or to allow vulnerability. I know some people don't ever want any such tools, they don't want anything to access the dark and repressed information in their buffers, they prefer them to remain hidden, to keep sweeping that dirt under the carpet of their subconscious. But just like with a computer, when it goes too long without updates and disk/anti-virus scans, errors and problems keep accumulating to the point of crashes and lost data. It takes courage to do that for ourselves, and also to be there for others, to help them through their own stuff. Not doing that, the whole world suffers for it, not only the people concerned, but everyone around them as well, and it has a snowball effect. One angry person at work lowers the "vibe" for everyone else, same as in the household. Then those co-workers affected by that one angry/negative person take that home to their own family, to their spouses, to their children, and they carry it elsewhere. So, for all of us to do our part, is to free ourselves from everything that burdens us, that negatively affects our feelings and emotions and contributes to a lesser existence for everyone.

So by re-writing the past, we also re-write our future. To lessen the pain associated with our past, our trauma, our conditioning, racism, greed, narcissism, violence, is to lessen those things in our future as well, can we not all see that?

"Your transformation affects the world. If you as a human being transform yourself, you affect the consciousness of the rest of the world..." – **Jiddu Krishnamurti**

We hold on to so much pain from our past, and that pain will always be projected into our future in equal measure, there is no other way things can be. For every action, and for all energy, an equal reaction must take place. For all the pain we keep alive in us, that we maintain, all that energy must keep rolling on into our future, it doesn't stay contained in your being, it always seeps out through every pore and orifice at the energy level, in how you act, how you behave, what you say, and what you don't say. So collectively, we all share a responsibility for the level or racism that persists, terrorism, materialism, poverty, abuse, human trafficking... Where does it stop? When people look into their own backyards with more scrutiny, their interior selves, and stop blaming, stop being ashamed of who they are, and to go beyond the fear of finding out the amount of racism, greed, trauma and such they have within themselves.

Living Life in Survival Mode

The interactions between our mind and emotions is a complex process, and also our fears, our lower animal traits that can still overrun our system, the chemicals that trigger all sorts of responses, all control our lives much more than we realize. Which is why I believe humanity must work towards a better understanding of trauma, the stuff that gets stuck in our system, and emotional maturity, to overcome our animal response behaviors. And if successful, this might start a new era for humanity perhaps... This animal response system is very much responsible for keeping us separated from one another, always fearful of predators or invaders, anyone who would steal our resources, kill us, or take over our tribe. We are still living that reality in most countries, accumulating resources, protecting them, fending off against invaders, and fighting for other resources as needed. That is not the best that humanity can do, love is about sharing, community, inclusivity. **That is why some people can be**

tremendously happy with nothing, and others so miserable with plenty. To become a master of your emotional domain, is to take control of those reactions, so that you don't spend your life chasing things you don't really want or need, or keep running away from things you actually *do* want. Living the way of the animal, every tribe for themselves, you cannot help but to have military, wars, conflicts, fighting for resources, that will never end. Unfortunately, even though people might have deep down within themselves the desire for healthy and supportive communities, the way our societies are built, they compel people towards individualism, to accumulate resources, and to fight to maintain them. The down side of this; less love to go around, seeing everyone as an enemy or a resource to exploit, and living life in a very poor way. Again, being careful of judgments, knowing that what we do, we do for various reasons, and many are complicated to understand, and many are conditioning from the societies that we have built. Some solutions might be easy to say, but not so easy to implement, I get that, it is in the effort that we shall find our light.

"There came a time when the risk to remain tight in the bud was more painful than the risk it took to blossom..."
– Anaïs Nin

So, we do have all sorts of fears that push us to neglect our inner emotional and psychological landscapes, and many of those fears have their origins from way back in our past, from when we were animals trying not to get kicked out of the herd, and not eaten, or fall out of tress, or cliffs. We don't need those fears anymore for the most part at least, but there they are regardless for us to contend with. And if we don't become aware of them, they will keep ruling over us until we do.

The Crazy Things we do just to Belong

Unfortunately a lot of our fears of not belonging, getting "cast out", rejected, again comes from way back in our past, when being cast out of the tribe/herd meant death... Our animal nature, our prehistoric days, not belonging meant facing the jungle on our own, being picked off by predators, killed by other tribes, dying of starvation, or even loneliness. Today we don't need those fears to keep us within a certain tribe, we don't need to repress our true selves, our best gifts, to not offend anyone by fear of being singled out or killed from jealousy or fear.

"I know it hurts. I know you feel like you weren't good enough. But your breakthrough is coming. Don't give up on yourself now. You came too far. Your value is still high and you're still beautiful. You don't need anyone to claim you to feel whole. Let it hurt and grow from it..."
– Keishorne Scott

The fear of being alone, abandoned, might be the most powerful fear that we have, it drives us in so many unseen ways, yet it is mostly redundant nowadays. Yes, we do need a social life, to connect with others, but we can get that rather easily, if not for deeper connections that we all crave, at least on a superficial level, or half superficial. We can go out to restaurants on our own, do so many things, get engaged in various groups, join a host of gyms and sporting activities, community, surrounded by co-workers and such. Not to say it is easy making good friends and be in loving relationships, often our character differences makes it hard, but at least we don't need to "fear" rejection, as abandonment from anyone will not result in our death, we can survive quite well on our own, thrive even.

Yes, again, we do need deeper connections in our lives for us to feel good about ourselves, to feel appreciated, to recharge. But

126

even when surrounded by people, most don't get that anyway, and a lot of those crazy things we do to belong are not only wasted because they don't give us what we truly need, we become someone else along the way. Our capacity to connect and belong is very much related to how well we know ourselves, and our level of healing. Some people can do almost anything to "blend in", everything except being themselves, and suffer the consequences. And besides, if you were to find love, would you rather be loved for who you really are, or for whoever you let yourself become out of your needs to fit in?

"Trying to build your life living through the Ego and Ega, the faces we put on for show and acceptance, is a bit like trying to build a castle on clouds, the stones keep falling through, accumulating into a pile of rubble underneath..." – Me

Unfortunately, as life becomes more complicated and fast paced, it becomes increasingly difficult to truly belong anywhere, to anyone. Belonging requires deeper connections, deeper knowledge, not only of others, but of ourselves as well. One of the major aspects of the relationship between belonging and healing, is that **the more you heal, the more your sense of belonging comes from deep within you.** And also, you become a lot more compatible to everyone, belonging with others becomes a lot easier, and you can choose how and who to belong with. So no need to do drugs, to smoke, to dress all weird or all muted, to act a certain way, to hide yourself behind walls of conformity. No need to repress your sense of expression from fears that people will judge you, no need to jump through so many hoops, afraid that people will not like you as you are. When you belong to yourself at a deep enough level, then you belong to the world as well, and that sense of belonging carries you through life.

"Persons of high self-esteem are not driven to make themselves superior to others; they do not seek to prove their value by measuring themselves against a comparative

standard. Their joy is being who they are, not in being better than someone else..." – **Nathaniel Branden**

If people understood everything that they do in life specifically from their need of belonging, all the negative repercussions it has not only in their external surroundings and path, but also in how deeply repressing to their own true selves they have become, it might just bring them to tears. All that stuff in our repressed systems, our Ego and Ega, make us feel alone and unlovable, which is why we often prevent ourselves from looking into those things, out of shame and embarrassment, and also out of fear that if we acknowledge the presence of all of that darkness we will surely be rejected and abandoned for it.

Every time we choose belonging instead of authenticity, we add one more stone on the back of our true selves, pushing it further down in the depth of our subconscious. Every one of those stones will need to be uncovered, processed and let go of before we can reclaim our true self. And in a sad way, all of what we do to belong usually doesn't add to much in our lives. As to truly satisfy that need of belonging, it must come from our true self, yet we keep repressing it in the hopes that people will like us more, ironic isn't it?

SIDE NOTE: Be careful of the "everybody's doing it" excuse. Many people excuse themselves of their behaviors by thinking well, "everyone" is doing it, why not me? But those are often false perceptions that can be very self-serving at times. Just like when you buy a car, and suddenly your brain starts picking up on all other similar cars on the road, and then you think "everyone" has the same car as you. Nope, just your brain seeing what it wants to see. So human traffickers, drug dealers, thieves, tax evaders, abusive and selfish people, they can all make themselves feel better by only focusing on others like them, and thinking they are part of the "norm", so why change? Not to say this process is the biggest part of it, but it gives people an excuse to keep doing things that they know are morally reprehensible. And then the ego kicks in, if I don't do it, then someone else will, or I will be at a disadvantage, I will lose. This "everyone else is doing it" notion that we convince ourselves of is responsible for many of our ills, even for stealing a pen at work, littering, or not picking up litter as "no one else is either", which is part of the same principle. We judge ourselves too much by what others do or don't do, and allow ourselves to become that which we know is not the best that we can do, but it is often the easier path that we fall into.

AS A PRACTICE: Take some time to consider what you might be sacrificing of your truer self for the sake of being accepted either at work, with family or friends, or in a relationship. Do you feel like you would be judged if you acted in a way that felt more "you", if you pointed out hurtful behaviors of others, if you felt like singing out but don't. In all kinds of ways we put our "self" aside because we are made to feel as if we should, or judged/ridiculed into becoming someone else. Do you feel as if you act in false ways at times, laugh at jokes that you find are rude or impolite just to be like the others. Think of an environment that you feel makes more sense to you, where you would be comfortable with all the conversations, the humor, the activities. What changes do you think you can make that can bring you there, joining a group, maybe moving to a different part of the city, or a different city/country even. Maybe a place where people keep active more regularly, instead of sitting in bars and drinking, to surround yourself with the details that make you feel better about who you are, and how you need to express yourself. Yes, again, the details add up. If you live in a part of a city surrounded by sports bars and fast food joints, but you prefer small coffee shops, yoga studios and healthy foods, well, everyone that you cross paths with on a daily basis, all interactions, whether verbal or not, add up to how you feel at the end of the week, drained, or uplifted, in harmony with your environment, or at odds with it. We get so lost in the little details that we think are not important, it does all add up in the end. How much of those little details are aligned with your greater life story? Take some time to consider all of it, the balance, and make a plan to improve upon them. To make changes towards tweaking some of those details so that they feel more in tune with how you see yourself down the road.

All of your Feelings are Valid, do not Dismiss any of them

One of the difficulties in making progress in life, for healing, E.M., love, is that for a while, you will need to consider much of your behaviors, your actions, and your reactions, and persistently make some efforts to choose the best alternative. So, to be in the habit of always observing our reactions can be a bit tedious, but it is necessary, otherwise how can you expect to make progress? To step out from your old reactions, is to step out of your old wounds, to look at them, and say, I can do better. I choose to not react in that way anymore. I choose to not get pissed off if someone cuts me off, yeah, maybe the person is a jerk, maybe they are selfish, maybe they have an important meeting and their child needed a bit of extra time that morning, who knows, but I choose to not get pissed off no matter the reason. I will let go of this sense of "entitlement" to negative emotions. That is how we make progress, by consistently choosing compassion and empathy over anything else.

But, keep in mind that this does not mean to brush off your feelings about what is going on, on the contrary, it is to feel all of it, consider, and choose the better alternatives. The more we understand ourselves from deep within, the more we realize how much our lives can improve by cleaning up those nasty dysfunctional storage places that our unprocessed emotions and experiences end up in. Remember, our systems are indeed intelligent, but, if "you", the controller, the maestro, cannot use all of your knowledge and capacities to properly process your present experiences, your system cannot reconcile within itself faulty and unbalanced information of any sort. If it cannot process it, it cannot either integrate it properly, or "throw it out" either, so it gets stuck somewhere in your being.

Your ability to heal is very much related to your ability to feel the right feelings your body is trying to convey to you, the right feelings the situation calls for. **So never dismiss, judge, ridicule, oppress, run away from, or repress your feelings.** Also, do not allow anyone else to do those things to you either. And also to realize that to heal, is to first *feel* the wounds and blocked stuff that lie dormant within us, then we start to really understand that we will need to feel lots of things as we proceed along this path, and many of those things will not be pleasant to experience. But, getting in touch with our feelings does not give us the right to lash out at people though. Knowing your feelings, and allowing them to rise out of your body doesn't give you a "carte blanche" to hit other people on the head with them...

Accepting your feelings, or the feelings of others, and talking out/expressing them is not a free pass to abuse, yell, or hurt anyone, or accept that of others. Do not allow yourself to "throw" your feelings at others. If you feel jealous, simply say you feel jealous and why, and seek a way of getting over those feelings in a healthy way. Feeling your emotions is one thing, but blaming others for those feelings is mostly not advisable, unless you are really sure that they actually are the main cause of your current feelings. Yes, blame can be therapeutic in *some situations*, but it is a tricky thing to indulge in. Healthy blame and angering is crucial for proper healing, and freeing your system of negative blockages for love and compassion to take its place. Though the scope of this process far surpasses the expectations of this book (I do come back a little on this later), but there are plenty of resources for you to find out more. The idea to consider is how best to get in touch with your true feelings, and the barriers that prevent them from surfacing, or twisting them into all sorts of things that aren't so pretty to look at.

Life Spent Avoiding our Fears, Instead of Following our Dreams

This is another damaging aspect of our Dysfunctional Emotional/Mind Matrices...

We often spend much more time avoiding the things that trigger our unconscious trauma and dysfunctional programming, that power up our Matrix, instead of going towards the things we really would like to have in our lives. We might spend 90% of our lives directing our path in a way that avoids the trauma in our subconscious, or going after desires that are also based on our conditioning, rather than living a life that pulls us towards love and happiness. And if you take a good look around, at how people spend the bulk of their time, it is not so hard to confirm this sentiment. How many people are truly happy with all aspects of their lives, that feel every day is like a gift to them, living mostly in bliss and contentment? Not many unfortunately...

I don't believe for one instant that that is just how humans are meant to be, the only existence they can ever hope for. If an average person would be connected to some kind of device that monitored every minute of their emotional state for one week, how many of those minutes would be "very happy", and how many would be stress, anxiety, concerns, fears, frustrations... Think of a normal work week, getting up groggy, depleted, not wanting to go to work, breakfast, traffic, boss, co-workers, heavy work load, hoping for something better, traffic coming back home, supper, relationship issues, family... That is "normal" for many people. We choose our lives based on our pain body/mind for the most part, not willingly, but by default and lack of awareness. Most of our life is about avoiding the pain, the blockages, the faulty programming, which is a sad way of living, actually, it is not "living" at all, it is just a slow decline towards death.

> *"Life is not about waiting for the storms to pass. It's about learning how to dance in the rain..."* – **Vivian Greene**

Consider your soul as a being of energy, and it seeks to interface with your human body at the maximum potential, and there are two main components, two main interfaces, the mind and the body, thoughts and emotions. Now, all trauma, dysfunctional conditioning, programming, judgments, shame, guilt, jealousy, anger, all of those things are impediments to this interfacing process. Your soul is as close to love as you can get, and through your soul also comes the deepest and truest connection to the creation itself. So, what are you willing to do to make it happen? To remove all impurities that prevent your soul from interfacing with your physical being, to have the best life possible, the most love, to be fully integrated in all possible ways, to be fully alive...

I believe we are capable of much more, but we do need to take some time out, and plant those seeds that will take us to a better future.

Now think about this: If "everyone" is in the same boat, if everyone spends more time avoiding the pain in their subconscious rather than striving towards love and purpose, then our whole world gets created by that pain, as every decision, every action, comes more from pain than from love, and all that we build along the way corresponds more to our fears, instead of our loving nature. This gives you an idea of why the world is the way it is, how societies get built, why there is still so much poverty, wars, conflicts, abuse... The ill effects are exponential and get passed on from one generation to the next, it becomes the history we then fight against.

A fully healed person paints the world around them in love, and an unhealed person in fear, simple as that. The world can only change when we reduce our trauma, or "pain bodies", when we choose to do what is necessary to pull us out of the illusions we live in, to take those red pills as often as we need to, which will keep increasing our capacity to love, to be present. But if only a few take on this great responsibility, then the world cannot change. Technology will advance, civilizations will rise and fall, but the balance of suffering will remain the same.

SIDE NOTE: Speaking of great battles, consider this one... ***"Hugs and kisses; the real war on drugs that we need..."***. Think about this: A child that does not get the attention they need, which puts them in a "deficit of attention" state, will then grow up to have "attention deficit", and isn't that how it goes? The more parents become busy with all sorts of things, the more they neglect the true needs of their children, which is a lot of love, compassion, care, healthy interaction on a daily basis, then with those lacks, the more there are people with attention deficit disorders of all types. The solution is not to keep medicating, the solution is to hug and kiss more, literally, but also with words and caring. A smartphone, computer, games, social media, are all ill replacements for the true connectedness that a growing child needs to create healthy connections within themselves, and without those healthy connections, focusing and being present becomes increasingly difficult. I don't think it's a coincidence that attention deficit seems to follow an inverse path to the decline of family suppers and simple activities of quality time spent together.

Again, it's a complicated world we have created, no easy solutions, but that doesn't mean we shouldn't try. And yes, learning about ourselves can seem as complicated as the world we have created, but you already knew that, as most people know how complicated it can be just to understand the one person they have, or had, a relationship with.

Sometimes its a roller coaster, other times a desert, a joyful vacation, or tedious work, rain, snow, happiness, rejection...

Love yourself, take it easy, enjoy the ride!

Intermission

Just like the plays of old, here is an intermission, to take a step back, contemplate, and get a bit of a grasp on what has gone on in the first half... Go to the bathroom, make yourself some popcorn, or a nice cup of tea, maybe get some fresh air, cuddle with someone close if you can, to come back more relaxed and eager to explore a bit more.

How much of your attention have I managed to get so far?

I don't expect all of it, we are human after all, but at least enough to get you to focus more profoundly on certain aspects of yourself, to understand at a deeper level, and expand beyond your current programming. Through it all, keep in mind that you can't always control what happens to you, but you can always control how you react and behave, your thoughts, your actions, your words. That is how we become emotionally mature, to *choose* love and compassion as much as humanly possible when choices need to be made.

So, keep in mind that these are a few steps along your path, of many that you will need to take to truly make your life splendid. I hope this will provide you with tools that will take you closer to that reality.

The next half is more practical in nature, elaborating on some of the things in the first half, plus more examples and exercises to apply in your daily life, so that all you have learned will not only stay in your mind, but will become part of your being as a whole. As we are all stories in the making, choose wisely how you take those steps to a better ending.

PART 2: Life as a Love Letter

Do you ever get the feeling that life is just not what it should be for you?

You look around, maybe not too bad, a good job, friends, family, but still, that nagging feeling in the bottom of your heart that comes up once in a while saying something is not quite right. But you push it back down, convincing yourself that your life is "good enough", and that you should not complain, or that some day it will get better. But it comes back, maybe six months later, maybe a few years, whatever the frequency, it never goes away completely. During which time you distracted yourself, chased a few more goals, took care of your daily living, changed a few things here and there. But there it is again, like a surreal feeling, despite what your brain sees, your heart is crying out that this is not the life meant for you, somehow, it just isn't. Even if you think you have "everything" you need, something just isn't right.

Well, that is your heart, your soul talking to you, and the clock is ticking, your chances of finally setting your life on a better path are dwindling. And that feeling, you shouldn't keep dismissing it, instead you should ask it what it wants from you, and you should really hope that it answers. It can be your greatest guide to finally getting to that better life. And by better, I do mean more love, more purpose, closer to what you would call a "dream life" full of lasting joy and happiness. Even if the life you have now is good enough, family, dwelling, career and such, most people would say they are far away from a dream life, and a lot has to do with them not even knowing what that life could be. And that comes from not knowing who they really are in the first place, what they're made of deep inside.

"It is worth remembering that the time of greatest gain in terms of wisdom and inner strength is often that of greatest difficulty..." – **Dalai Lama**

Make no mistake of it, all this work, everything that you do to heal, to overcome your trauma, to increase your emotional maturity, it is indeed a true labor of love for yourself. All part of your best efforts at a sort of love letter, your greatest story, manifested as the journey you undertake in life. To ultimately live your life as your true self, and not through the fears and conditioning of the past, not through the soul depriving dysfunctional programming, but to go beyond all the unsaid words and unexpressed emotions and feelings, to free your being from all the stuff that impedes its natural expression, that keeps it at bay from all the things it, you, desire most.

That's the real work that matters most for anyone, the goal above all other goals in life. Don't keep spending your valuable time lost in the little details, the smaller goals that seem to always take over, don't wait until your time has run out to get to what you truly want, and deserve.

Taking a few Steps Back

Before we dive heart first into this second half, I wanted to take some time and reiterate a few sentiments I shared in the first part of the book. I know I can be very direct at times, I poke, I prod, I use humor, and maybe even a tinge of teasing... But, I wanted you all to know I take trauma and unhappiness very seriously, and all the suffering and unhealthy conditioning we carry, otherwise I would not be writing this book, and I would not have sacrificed so much in my life to understand it, not just for me, but for you as well.

I greatly empathize with the pain you are carrying, all of you, no matter where that pain comes from, and no matter what that pain has caused you to do, even the stuff you aren't even aware of. Narcissists, psychopaths, abusive people, all those that have become repressed, full of suffering, and how you needed to disconnect from that suffering because you were not able to deal with it, I still feel for you, I do. I have experienced it numerous times, to see how hurtful people have been to me (and some of what I passed on to others), but also knowing that they only did it for the pain they themselves were carrying, and often had no clue how to deal with.

Yes, I, and we, need to protect ourselves from the pain some might inflict, crimes must be punished by whatever laws we have created for them. **But we are *all* human deep down**, and those that are the most violent and hateful, are often the ones with the most pain, and unfortunately they behave in ways that people want to run away from. I get that, and even though you might be all prickly on the outside, full of armor and weapons, on the inside all you want is a great big hug. But again, unfortunately you might go through the rest of your life guarded, never allowing yourself to even realize you just want to be hugged like everyone else.

And this goes for all of us, we all more or less have numerous guards that we hold up against the world, against anyone who might want to harm us, or even love us, and we all cause harm to others at times, the idea is to reduce the pain we carry, not to assume we'll rid ourselves entirely of it.

And for all the other people that fall mostly in the general population, hurt, but not to the point of causing violence and excessive abuse to others, I feel for you as well. I know, so much of the "normal" pain we have can seem trivial to us at times when compared to some of the abuse others have endured, but still we must not dismiss it. It is not because someone else has suffered more, that you just have to find a way to deal with your pain on your own. That thinking will only lead us on the path where there is only one human on this planet at any one time who would be allowed to cry out their suffering, the one that has suffered most beyond all others and would have no one else that has suffered more to keep them quiet, which is complete nonsense.

I wish I had the strength, the words, the know how to make all of it stop, to help people get over it, to find a way that would remove the taboos surrounding all of it, to lift the shame, the embarrassment, to have people not see themselves as to blame for what happened to them, to make it something that people are willing to talk about, to get it out of their systems. The more it remains in the shadows, as dirty little family secrets, or shameful things best left unsaid, as things we should never mention for whatever reasons, or because others have it worse. Well, to always keep up the appearance we are all well on the inside, the less our chances of healing humanity from those sufferings.

> *"Beautiful are those whose brokenness gives birth to transformation and wisdom..."* – **John Mark Green**

We keep focusing on technological advances, climate, cell phone coverage, internet, electric cars, pollution... But what about us?

Shouldn't *we* be the most important things to focus on? How can we keep thinking about the economy and politics when we know very well how many people are suffering in the background. For some people in charge, seems like all they are interested in is to know that most people are "well enough" to contribute their share to the economy and work force. If they break down along the way, they'll just replace them with others that are well enough to do the job, as if we're just interchangeable parts for them. To me, that is how we treated work horses in the old days, not how we should treat people, we should know better. **What efforts are made today to stop the abuse *before* it happens?** What are we doing to resolve the deeper issues other than finding a new drug to mask them? Seems like we are allowing parents to do whatever they want to their children (or corporations and governments to their citizens), as if we are saying it is their right to abuse their offspring, as long as we don't know what is going on, as long as the abuse is not reported, or the injuries don't require hospitalization, we'll just keep turning a blind eye to it. And for people in general, we so often dismiss their psychological and emotional well being in favor of productivity and appearances, "the show must go on" kind of attitude while people become more depressed and stressed out, exhausted and disillusioned. For me, that is not good enough, I am limited in what I can do, but at least I can try something.

Again, no matter what I say, and no matter how I say it in my attempts to poke you into taking your own suffering and your love for yourself more seriously, I share your pain and I sincerely hope to be of help to free you from at least some of it. Be kind to yourself, and be compassionate to others. We all have pain, we all have experienced sorrows, and we all have dysfunctional programming and sometimes wacky emotional systems that makes it hard for us to trust others, to be vulnerable enough to allow ourselves to dream of a better existence, to live more free and truer to our best selves.

Now off we go into the second half parts, I've got more idealism to share, stories, good info and exercises, great quotes, and a bit more caring poking and compassionate support that I must attend to:) But before we start, let's just take a moment and call truce to all of our Ego's, our narcissism, our blame and selfishness, our impenetrable force fields and prickly exteriors, and give ourselves another hug shall we, really, I'm not kidding, hug yourself, like, right now!

Living your Life as if it was a Love Letter to Yourself

Wouldn't that be great?

If your life was like that, a story that resembled the best love letter to yourself you can come up with... The kind that you wish someone would write to you, about lifting you out of your every day life, whisking you off to some exotic place where all your worries and troubles would melt away in the distant background, any kind of problem you might have had, bad memories, all gone, pain just a very distant feeling from a long ago era.

This love letter would not only be about romantic love, partnership, but all the major details of your life, so, your whole life story. A story where your most important needs would be met, a deep sense of belonging enveloping you, waking up in the morning in a great mood and ready to face your day, purpose and passion replacing mundane and dreary habits and routines. No more struggling with finding your place in this world, no more feeling like an alien, no more longing for romance or love, for someone to rescue you from loneliness and an uneventful existence.

All of those feelings can come from within you, but I wouldn't say they can be there for you regardless of the situation you find yourself in. Poverty sucks, living on the streets, being physically unhealthy, stuck in a country at war. I understand that currently not everyone on this planet can know bliss if only they worked hard to heal and develop self-love. Many do not have their fundamental needs met, and until then, living any kind of life other than basic survival can be hard, or maybe even impossible. But for the most part, for people reading this book, they can move on to a path that can bring them to a much better life if they did that. It's not sorcery, work is required, time, dedication, awareness, just like with any other relationship that we value and want to develop. **Unfortunately people spend way more time trying to win, and keep, *other* people in their lives** because they know that if they don't, people can just walk away when things don't go well. But for us, we are stuck with ourselves, so we often take ourselves for granted. So no matter how badly we treat "us", we think we can never run away, at least on the physical level. Yet we do, in all of those parts of us that are not in the present, lost in the seas of our subconscious.

Love will come to you when you do the Things you Love

You know the idea, about not to "seek" love, it will find you when you start doing the things *you* love? Well, doing the things you love starts with becoming a loving person first, a person that loves *themselves*, and that is the most attractive quality anyone can have. Then when loving people start doing things that come from the love they have for themselves, they then start attracting back all of those lost parts, and they start attracting more people on the outside as well.

*On the flip side, as an opposition to living a life as a love letter, to put things in perspective: How does *"Functional Enough"* sound as your Epitaph? You know, those little sayings on tombstones that encompass what your life has been about, or what you leave behind... Is that what you want as a legacy, what your life story will be about?

Someone that is functional enough, as many people are, will never become a force to be reckoned with at anything. Holding a steady job, sure, maybe even buying a house perhaps, but not much more than that, not awesome, no true love, no greatness in any domain. Just functional enough to get by, while soothing whatever extra yearnings in entertainment and distractions. Is there room enough on this planet for everyone to be a shining light, I don't know, but why don't we try and find out?

"Love will find a way through paths where wolves fear to prey..." – **Lord Byron**

FOOD FOR THOUGHT: Sometimes you might feel like there is too much history and heartache for you ever to find your way back to the light, to love, and to happiness, but there's always time, well, until it runs out obviously. Though you must be willing to work on wiping the slate, to start over with baby steps, just like when you were very young, to re-learn what life is about, and who you are beyond all that accumulated stuff.

But the truth is, is that we do just that, we do run away so often, although not in a visible manner that we understand and see. And as long as we run from the important things, love can never catch up. Again, think of the previous sections, of how no one is whole on the inside. When we accept abuse, when we treat ourselves poorly, when we obsessively focus on career and work despite mounting stress and anxiety, **we neglect that one true relationship that we should cherish above all else, us.** And those parts of us that are bruised, fractured, traumatized, stuck in our systems waiting for us to notice, they know, they see, they understand how little attention and care you have for them. They are desperately waiting for you to stop turning a blind eye to their suffering, to stop walking the other way, and to finally give them the empathy and compassion they truly deserve. Money is not the answer, how do you feel if someone tries to buy your love with money? Well, if you yourself keep focusing on career objectives and finances, then it is as if you are saying that to yourself, you are trying to buy your own love with money,

144

instead of putting the time into building up a truly loving relationship.

So, when you are focusing on trying to retain those people around you that make you feel better on the outside (and oftentimes not so much), know that this *better feeling* you run after, you can have it always right from within you. The more you develop a relationship with those parts, to heal them, to show them you care, for them to want to make that journey out of the darkness and know you will be there for them when they finally reach the light, they will start providing you with that feeling, your wholeness will increase, and so will your feelings of belonging and purpose. Just like you, they are also waiting for a better life, waiting to know that their abusers are not there anymore, since in their world, living in the past, they think they still are. They want to know you have grown in courage, to ensure you will not let anyone else abuse you in the present, that you have understood what kind of life you need that is more loving, a more supportive and caring environment. All of it works together for building a more suitable home for you to grow in.

Oh, I'm reminded of a song...

MUSICAL INTERLUDE: *I Choose You*, by **Sara Bareilles** (Check out the "Live at the Manderley Bar" video version)

Telling the world that you've finally got it all right, something to hope for... (You'd know what this meant if you listened to the song;)

So, this *life as a love letter to yourself*, part of it is about gaining the trust of all of your parts, to let them know that you will do what they need to feel safe and treasured, to let them know you will be there through thick and thin, and that you are willing to make the changes necessary to make it happen.

That is the biggest promise you can make to yourself, to *all* of your "selves". Just like with a real lover, willing to sacrifice whatever for them, compromise, share in vulnerability and honesty, the best of relationships. And all the work to undo dysfunctional programming and conditioning as well, for having your whole environment support and promote health and wellbeing.

Accepting people who are abusive to you, and around you, even if only sarcasm or lack of vulnerability, can be detrimental to your own relationship, to your own love. Seeking out environments, people, situations, that make you feel safe, cared for, that you can allow yourself to be vulnerable, is extremely important, not just for healing, but for being able to open yourself up to deeper bonds, love, empathy... And the opposite is true, people and places that make you feel on guard, where you can't share your emotions, your vulnerabilities, will keep you in your trauma, in pain, in very shallow thoughts and feelings.

That doesn't sound like a life lived as a love letter, does it?

If you can't even allow yourself to be vulnerable around the people you currently spend most time with, how is that even remotely close to the kind of love you dream of? But the more you accept that as your reality, you will be forever postponing anything better. Do you want to keep living life as a prisoner, putting your time in, keeping your head low to not attract attention out of fear of what might happen to you? Letting other people dictate how much love and happiness you can have, all the while your best parts, your best gifts, are left to rust in the fields of your forgotten dreams...

Let's say it all together now, "Hell No!"

You need to have the courage to step out of the old, and leave those spaces empty for a while before the new can grace your life, allowing the soil to become fertile again. Don't think it will be an easy transition without the need for some painful changes/sacrifices, it doesn't work that way, so prepare yourselves for a bit of sorrowful times, as if grieving the life you never had. If you have a habit of running to unhealthy relationships or casual sex any time you feel low on yourself (or other unhealthy habits), you will need to first stop, then spend some time accepting those low moods and feelings without going back to your old patterns. To go through the pain despite how much it can hurt in order to prove to yourself that you have changed, and are willing to stick with the new program, this new life that is waiting for you on the other side of your efforts.

If you keep substituting one bad habit or unhealthy pattern for another, then what have you proven to yourself? There are a lot of things that we do in life that makes sense on paper, but in our hearts, it is far from the reality it exists in, and that is what we need to change. Dreams cannot come to life when your clouds are dark and stormy, nor can love find its way to you through tempestuous seas.

"The only way to deal with an unfree world is to become so absolutely free that your very existence is an act of rebellion..." – **Albert Camus**

THINK ABOUT THIS: If a person has a 10,000$ wine cellar, and has all kinds of pride and attachments to it, all of that space within him/her will prevent love from coming in. And that goes the same with other attachments, desires, and various dysfunctions. If that person replaces their wine cellar with an art collection, same thing. But if they rid themselves of it for the specific purpose of growing in self-love, and leaving those empty spaces within them for a period of time even if they feel a void, and holding the belief that in that void, love will eventually grow, then that is how we attract love into our lives. To not only heal for the love of ourselves, but to let go of all kinds of things that don't serve our higher purpose and to allocate those empty spaces for better things, even if we must endure temporary pain in the process. And also, the idea is not to let go of all the things we enjoy and become monks, once our self-love has grown, then we become much more adept at figuring out what we really want out of life, values and morals, purpose. So maybe that wine cellar might make its way back into our lives, but having the courage to let go of it for your own love, even if only temporary, that is how you can gain trust within yourself, how far you are willing to go. Romantic lovers sometimes ask for similar sacrifices from their partners, even if only temporary, to prove their love, how much they care, same principles apply to you, for you.

The Desires of our Hearts often Remain Unrequited

"Le coeur a ses raisons que la raison ne connaît point..."
– Blaise Pascal

This is another French expression to mean that the heart has its reasons that our sense of reason knows nothing about. But isn't that how we live life, always through our mind, our reasoning process, and the heart gets left out most of the time? Remember that our heart is associated to our emotions and to our feminine nature, to leave that out of the story of your life, well, how can love, how can dreams be possible?

When your heart compels you to do something, try to make it a habit of leaving your brain out of the decision making process as much as possible, as it will most likely lead you astray, as our mind often sides with fear, real, or imagined, as often is the case. But that doesn't mean to follow every whim of your emotions either, as the more fractured and dissociated we are, the more our emotional systems are filled with errors and dysfunctions, so without healing, those too can lead you astray.

The greater gap between our heart and mind, and the Ega and Ego, the less we can understand what our heart truly wants, and the more our mind will surrender to fears, as there is nothing for it to trust, no genuine feelings to base its decisions on. So your mind becomes selfish, or constantly evaluating pros and cons. When it feels an impulse from the heart, it asks "but what will that get me... Power, fortunes, a new car, a bigger house?". Then the answers comes back, "No", so then the mind goes, "No", and all remains the same in your life. The heart can compel us to do certain things, to follow certain paths, but it is our mind that allows it, and when the Ego is in full control, the picture of your life gets painted without much love and compassion in it. **To follow your heart even if it doesn't make sense to your brain**, that is how you can start to pull yourself out of your Ego, to heal, and to find the best path to your life. That is the feminine intuition we need to acquaint ourselves with, our internal compass that can guide us to all the unseen treasures that have eluded our grasp until then.

Your capacity to have the best life in your near future depends on how much you are willing to process of the past, of how much you can re-integrate of your fractured selves, and the sacrifices you are prepared to undertake to make it happen. And also, the more you fine tune your emotional system, the more you will develop a much better relationship with your feelings, and that is what you need to be guided to greatness, through the darkest of nights, and the stormiest of seas.

So this "love letter" to yourself, of course that for there to be true love, there must also be awareness, acceptance, empathy, caring... There is no such thing as "blind" love, love is not blind, not at all. *Love sees all, knows all, but cares nonetheless*, that is true love. So, to love yourself truly, you must know yourself truly, you must endeavor to become whole to yourself, and accept what you find on that path.

If you don't know your own heart, from one end of it to the other, how can you think you can manage to create a life that looks anything near to your dreams? How can you tell anyone that you truly love them, if you have not managed to truly love yourself? How can you be an example to your children if you have not become an example to yourself?

To Love is to Live...

Why again do we keep Accepting abusive Situations?

Some of you might have asked yourselves this at some point along the way, either before, or during the reading of this book. Why do we accept abuse, or abuse others, even if it is only verbal or other seemingly inconsequential maltreatment? Why don't we do more to heal, to overcome our trauma, why do we accept all sorts of things in our lives that pull us away from love, from happiness? Things that stress us, that prevents us from increasing our E.M., all that is unhealthy, foods, addictions, alcohol... This pool of abuse, of fears and dishonesty, why the heck do we go in it if it is so toxic? (Isn't that weird, 9 two letter words in a row, but it works...)

Deep down we all know we want to love, and be loved, and we all know we do many things that makes it so hard to get there, so, why?

That's a very good question, and if I could give you the perfect answer, it would be worthy of a Nobel Prize. But, even if there is no perfect explanation, it doesn't mean we should not ask, try, or at least give a partial one.

Well, for one, we often delude ourselves into thinking that there will always be a tomorrow to get whatever we don't have today. But that is not the case of course. And that pattern, of thinking that tomorrow will work out better, will make sure anything better will always remain out of reach, as tomorrow will always be tomorrow.

And also perceptions... When we are low in E.Q./E.M., we see the world, ourselves, others, through a very limited view. Those E-Glasses in disrepair, we just can't see our selfish, hurtful, self-absorbed behavior for what it is. Our fear of intimacy keeps us surrounded be people who are also afraid of intimacy, then we just engage in behaviors that make sense to us, drama, lies, deceit, sarcasm, pity, jealousy... Not so complicated, but the repercussions keep us in our pain, unhealthy patterns, prevents us from healing, and makes real love close to impossible. But, for those people, conditional love, love based on control, on material things, becomes the only kind of love they know, the only kind of love they can see at that time. So for them, that kind of love can be as "real" as true love, at least from their limited perspective. A person that has developed deep emotional maturity will see the difference, but not those that don't know anything else.

"I've never seen any life transformation that didn't begin with the person in question finally getting tired of their own nonsense..." – **Elizabeth Gilbert**

And the more we surrender to conditional love, to lower E.M. behaviors, the more unhealthy the exchanges of energies get for us. When you engage in unhealthy energies, unhealthy thoughts and actions, then that is what comes back to you, those are the laws of the universe we live in. And to grow in E.M., we pull away from those unhealthy energy exchanges, those bonds that are so detrimental to us. So it always goes back to our pain, our trauma, the things inside of us that prevent us from being truly, deeply, loving beings all the way down to our core.

Then why can't we stop acting from our pain? That is where the complications arise. Our trauma gets mixed up with all sorts of things, our actions, no matter how loving they start off as deep within, must go through all sorts of jagged hoops, twisted mirrors, judgments, fears, misguided hopes and so many other things, that by the time they get expressed into words and actions, they are often so distant from where they started that they look nothing like what they were when they began. And also, our inner systems often get stuck in loops, always scanning the environment for anything that might cause us harm, and again, misinterpreting much of what we see into things that are more threatening than what they actually are, which again, distances us from love, creates a multitude of barriers against it.

AN EXAMPLE: A man who beats his wife, that punch might have started deep within as a very honest attempt to "connect" in a loving way, but that man, so full of pain and misery, by the time it comes out, it is expressed with his fists instead of loving words. Can he not prevent himself from that? He could, if he healed the things that twisted the loving desires into physical violence, or have more strength not to surrender to them. Our trauma alters our sense of reality, it can make a punch look not so bad, as if the other person is deserving of it, or other reasons. And the person receiving it might buy into the lie, that they deserve it, because of their own trauma. This is more of an extreme example, but we can apply the same principle to almost everything that we do. Our sense of reality depends on how much trauma and dysfunctional programming we contain, whether we see a punch for the violent action it is, or if we see it as a deserving blow, that is determined by our conditioning, the things we experienced in life, and how those things shaped us along the way.

"People see what they want to see and what people want to see never has anything to do with the truth..."
– Roberto Bolaño

Although I don't agree with the "*never*", but to a great extent, yes, that is how we live our lives, and a lot of it has to do with the things inside of us we don't want to face, and how those things are responsible for creating our whole reality, and what we accept of it.

Think of your inner self, burdened by all your pain and trauma, every time it wants to express its beauty in the world, it must go through all the things you experienced but have not healed, plus all your judgments, racism, fears, repressed desires and all, not even going into the complicated existence we live in at the moment. Think of this inner self as your true nature, your soul, an exquisite being of light that must go through forests full of overgrown trees and bushes, swamps, dark caves, oil sands and such. This inner being might want to be a singer, to help people, to express beauty, but by the time that expression comes out, by the time your inner being gets out, it is full of bruises and scratches, funky smelling seaweed, patches of tar, bugs, open sores... Again, an exaggeration, but I find them rather useful to explore myself, and to help others do the same. That is why most people never get to have their "dream life", **not because they can't have one**, but because we unfortunately still understand so little about our emotions, our internal selves, and the stuff we do understand, we are often too afraid to face it.

So in that sense, those with very low E.M. might know to a certain extent the pain of what they do, and what others do to them, but they think that that is just how life is, so better just find ways of coping with the pain. That is why the lower a person has in E.M., the more prone to very unhealthy behaviors they get; addictions, drugs, over-eating, alcohol problems, violence in relationships... It is not because they don't *want* to change, it is often because they *can't*, or don't know where to start, it all seems overwhelming, like there is no way out. That is until they realize that the path out of their misery can only be had by healing, by increasing their E.M., and getting out of low E.M./abusive environments. And until people get a taste for the kind of love that is above and beyond the experiences they've spent their lives living, making sacrifices for something that they don't yet know can be very difficult.

LITTLE DISCLAIMER: So, I say that your true self must go through all of your dysfunctions and programming before it can express itself out into the world. That is *not* to say that it *always* has to be that way. In certain situations we can temporarily overcome our trauma and conditioning, fears and all, and express our truer nature through them, but that requires strength, courage, and a lot of love and compassion. Most of the time we don't, but we can. So when situations come along where you have a choice to overcome your trauma and fears and express something deeper, grab it and hold on tight, those are the times when you can grow in leaps and bounds. As long as you *choose* love and cast aside your fears in those situations, then you can heal a great deal in short amounts of time. Like for instance, finally standing up at a work meeting and bringing to the table for discussion the lunch thief, and "demanding" that a solution be found, even if some people dismiss the importance of it and just say to get over it. Not talking about it because some ridicule or disparage those that stand up for their rights, well, often in those situations we allow "evil" to win the little battles, the small details, and when the little battles are lost, the big ones often follow the same path, and that goes for you on the inside as well. Love, emotional maturity, those are your biggest allies in developing strength to stand up for your rights, to be counted, drawing the line to end the abuses... When your courage and understanding increases, you will start to get this at a deeper level and might actually want to seek out such growth opportunities, something to keep in mind.

Putting your "self" aside for Another, Including You

So then, how to take those first steps out of the dreadful dysfunctional conditioning and programming, the illusionary Matrices of our Ego and Ega?

Again, like almost everything, it all seems like a terrible joke played on us all, unending "catch 22's" all over the place. Like, by the time you realize you are in a deep depression, all of your energy is spent just surviving, and hardly anything is left to do anything about it. Or by the time you realize you are in an abusive relationship, the abuse drains you so much, keeps you in fear, that you don't know how to get out of it. Small steps, slowly changing your environment, the people you spend time with, the books you read, the shows you watch, the music you listen to, not tolerating even small amounts of abusive behaviors from people, learning how to draw a line... All adds up over time, so patience is required.

"To believe in something greater than you are might be the best gift you can give yourself in life, and in love..." – **Me**

When you start considering all of it, the work, the struggle, the pain, going through our fears, you might think, why?

If it is all about us, individually, then not only can it appear to be self-serving in the end, as the connection to how the world can improve along with *us* might not be so easy to understand and see. Even though many great people have said it, still, until you personally connect to it, understand it, it can all seem like nice words without so much substance. Especially if you just keep on working your regular day job, if you don't have a family, or not even be in a romantic relationship. I've been there, I get it, why try to make myself into a "greater person", all that work, if only to be a bit happier by yourself in the end, or in a small group? Not that happiness and self-love are not worth it, but, if I myself didn't feel that there was a greater reason to be better, then what was I doing it for, just for my little old self?

What other option was there though, giving up, accepting the delusions I knew had been the mainstay of my life until then? I was stuck for a while, trying to find a good reason to keep going after all the truths that I had connected with. Like taking that red pill, the Movie version, knowing the reality of it, but not having a team waiting on the other side to guide you in your new life. That's kind of how it felt, until I reconnected to my deeper beliefs. So for me, what helped when I reached rock bottom, when I felt the ground beneath my feet was at its lowest and there was no more caving in possible, was my belief in God, my soul, in a greater purpose of life, to believe in a healthier outcome for humanity. If you believe in that, or something similar, its a great place to start, if not, **then I suggest finding something greater than you are to believe in**, to *want* to make yourself the best that you can for.

Just think of something that you might want to become a force to be reckoned with in whatever this "thing" you choose to dedicate yourself to. To fight against sexual abuse, poverty, human trafficking, pollution, a worthy cause, suicide hot-line, being a big brother/sister... Even just playing a small part in those things, **as long as it makes you feel that the fight is not just about you**, or your confined social circle.

"Rock bottom became the solid foundation in which I rebuilt my life..." – **J.K. Rowling**

Not only does aiming for a greater purpose can fill you up with strength and motivation, it can greatly help you on your healing journey. To help heal, to pull you out of your trauma, to give you something high to reach for, something to hang onto when the times get tough. Like sending out a message to the universe, to the very structures of everything that exists, the energy that connects every one of us, the creation itself. This message is one that is not selfish, you are not asking to heal just so that you can land your dream job, tons of money, power or fame, but to help others.

That "self" sacrifice, again, does not mean to deplete yourself, to not be happy, to not have enough to ensure a good life, a house, those kinds of things. **But, this love and happiness you seek, is not to confine it to your own personal use, but to spread it back out into the world at large.** And I believe that is the only way to go about it really. The universe, all matter and energy is connected, it lives in its own way, sentient, and why would "it" help anyone in a great way if all they want is to build up their own private treasures? That is the basis of the law of attraction. True, narcissists and sociopaths can achieve big things without that kind of help, but it comes at a great cost to them, love becomes impossible, so does lasting happiness. The satisfaction they get can only come with conquest and control, relationships with friends and family will always be based on selfish motives, is that how you want to live? I sure the heck don't...

So, building up E.M., love, healing, all with a greater cause in mind, that is magic in the making!

"Life is never made unbearable by circumstances, but only by lack of meaning and purpose..." – **Victor Frankl**

So that is what I mean, putting yourself aside, even to you. Not to dismiss your needs, not to give all your money to the poor, and completely go without some of the "finer" things in life. But to keep in mind that you want to become the best version of yourself so that you can provide the biggest amount of help to a cause that you hold close to your heart. So that you can become that "force to be reckoned with" in your pursuit of justice, ending human trafficking, helping people overcome depression and suicidal thoughts, or smaller things, whatever seems right for you. And for that, you must become the best version of yourself to make it happen, to love, and be the happiest that you can be.

Wouldn't that fit quite nicely into the **"Living your Life as a Love Letter to Yourself"** idea?

And that special thing that would drive you forward, that might seem like just the right fit for you, for your life of purpose, it often comes back to your own personal experiences, the pains you, or someone close, have endured. And uncovering that is another one of those benefits of seeking a healing journey, and why purpose and meaning can only come with knowing yourself better. And of course, it doesn't have to be an Earth shattering thing, those examples are just the regular "go to" grand achievements, like curing cancer. It can be much more simple, as long as it makes sense to you.

So this putting aside of our "selves", think about it as putting aside your Ego really, your pain, your dysfunctional parts, as those are the parts of us that prevent us from naturally wanting to help others, the parts you don't want in your life anyway. Which is still quite hard to do, very hard, but again, the more you heal, the more you develop love, the easier it gets. And of course, by putting aside those parts, it is to heal, to let go and overcome, *not* to repress or control.

A lot of what stops us in our tracks has to do with our fears of getting hurt, emotionally, or being judged or rejected. Which is something we need to get over, and by becoming more vulnerable, you will experience hurt, but you can grow out of that hurt. To grow, your heart needs to crack, and heal, like building up any other muscle, the energy of love kind of works the same way. Our fears of getting hurt are way worse than we imagine, than the reality of facing where those fears come from.

Finding the right people who will not ridicule your efforts, who will not only make you feel safe enough to be vulnerable, but will actually encourage you to do so is so important, to share those things of the past, to share your concerns and fears of your present situations. Who will encourage you to get out of abusive situations, to heal, to let go, who will encourage you to pursue your dreams, not being jealous, not keeping you in their misery for fears that they will need to face it themselves... Many people do that, their fears of facing their stuff will keep them wanting to surround themselves with people that are equally afraid, each supporting themselves to remain blind, an unwritten agreement, and, well, since that is the topic of the next section, I'll end the section on this note; *C Major...*

Finding your Tribe

"I used to think that the worst thing in life was to end up all alone. It's not. The worst thing in life is ending up with people who make you feel all alone..." – **Robin Williams**

As promised, easing into the lightness a bit more, right?

So now...

Finding your "tribe" can go a long way to help you overcome all sorts of less than stellar programming, to re-create your life, your path, towards a brighter outcome. No one is perfect, and you don't need to judge anyone, but being surrounded by people who are not actively seeking to get over their own stuff, who instead cast out their pain in all directions, can be very detrimental to those who want to stop doing that.

Finding your tribe has more to it than just hanging out with your co-workers for a beer on Friday nights, or joining a certain group with similar interests. If you are not regularly swimming in the kindred energies of people that want more out of life, growing in E.M., love, finding their own passion, how do you think they can help you find yours?

Consider this expression: *"Qui se ressemble, s'assemble..."*

That's a popular French expression, similar to "Birds of a feather, flock together". So, people that are alike tend to find each other and build relationships, and that makes sense obviously. So, if you want to have an idea of who you are, look around you, those that you get along with the most, which can be a great exercise. But, also understand that those that hang around together also *become* like one another. We don't just gravitate towards people like us, we also become like them the more we spend time together. So if you choose the wrong crowds, then you become like the wrong crowds.

To have any deep sense of belonging, first you must belong to yourself, and until you find a way to start pulling yourself out of the Matrix, your world of illusions, you cannot do that. Anyone fully integrated in their pain bodies will never feel they belong anywhere, and this can be seen very clearly with people that have strong anti-social personalities. The more in your pain, the less belonging, and the less belonging, the less love and happiness. So first, belong to yourself by understanding what you need to heal and pull yourself out of your Ego and Ega. Next, find people who have done, or are doing, the same, and have had at least some level of success. Then belonging will come naturally, no need to do anything special about it. Like for love, it cannot be forced, manipulated, or controlled. Which is why it is kind of difficult to get that deep need of belonging that we all crave for satisfied, it is not to be found outside of ourselves despite our efforts.

Then... If you are attempting to increase your E.M., to heal your wounds and trauma, chances are you might need to reconsider those that you hang around with. I have mentioned this in part before, about how to thoroughly consider your whole environment, to make changes, and this is one more way to consider *why* you need to make those changes, an extra incentive. That is a good reason why those that are on a healing journey should not get too involved with people that are not on that path. **Emotionally immature people tend to stagnate, to accept mediocrity, they abhor change, and they will not grow with you unless it is in their heart to do so.** Sooner or later, you *will* need to face that reality, so best to generally avoid people that have no interest in self-reflection, or any kind of healing or E.M. stuff.

When most people in your main social circle keep comparing themselves to others with their cars, houses, careers, salaries, vacation spots... Do you really think you can separate yourself from that inside of you, to not engage in that jealousy, greed, dysfunctional competitiveness? That it won't negatively affect you, it won't drag you down to that level. No matter how much organic lotion you lather on your skin, if you keep bathing in battery acid, you will suffer the ill effects of it one way or the other, it'll catch up to you. With people, you'll end up either being assimilated into the collective, your energy system plugged into theirs, or you will be constantly second guessing yourself, feeling like an alien, and not connecting with anyone.

So for a while, you might find that you don't quite fit in anywhere, as there is often a clear delineation between people with low E.M., and those with higher ones. So you might find yourself lost in that "delineation" for a period of time, but don't despair, you can use that down time to reflect deeper. As I have mentioned, there is pain involved in growth, and in processing your past, and going through a sort of "forced" period of isolation can help you to make great progress, despite the temporary loneliness involved.

The good news... The more you increase your E.M., the more you heal from your past, the more you work on building a better relationship with yourself, then of course, the more you will enjoy your own company. Not that you will not need anyone in your life anymore, we all need good social interaction and companionship, but in the times when you will be alone at home (or elsewhere), the place will not feel so empty, and you will enjoy your own presence at a greater degree.

"Someone I once loved gave me a box full of darkness. It took me years to understand that this, too, was a gift..."
— Mary Oliver

Another important reason to take this step seriously: Even though your E.M. might increase, even though you might be better able to identify behaviors of people with low E.Q./E.M., and might be more guarded, their words can still hurt. We might intellectually know they are not trying to be mean, or they don't really know what they are doing, but the emotional impact can be hard to mitigate, even if we have strong boundaries, so best to avoid them as much as possible, if not completely avoid physically, at least to not bond with them.

And the more there are people on this planet that become emotionally mature, who then shy away from emotionally immature people, the more it will give them an incentive to grow themselves, to be for their own good as well, so everyone wins in the end.

And, a bit of a warning, people in your social circle might actually resent the change you are trying to make, well, those with lower E.Q./E.M., and will likely fight against your change in many different ways, which can not only also be hurtful, but make your progress that much more difficult. And the old "Misery Loves Company" expression applies, some people that are stuck in their own misery like when others around them remain miserable, not only keeping them company, but also giving them an excuse not to face their misery for what it is.

*And finding your "tribe" is not *all* about people, but your environment as well. As mentioned before, the little details that make up your surroundings, all of them contribute to making you, you, how they all interact with your various energy systems. If you are a creative type, but live in a place surrounded by scientists and engineers, and all shops and businesses around your home are all about computers and technical stuff. Well, you will feel at odds with your environment, and your energetic system will *be* at odds with your environment, which makes internal/emotional progress more difficult. Again, in this situation, it's not that scientists and engineers are not good people, but if you need arts and museums in your life to be happy, and the whole environment that goes along with that to feel at home, then again, choose wisely.

How to spot high/low E.Q. People

Back to people: To find your tribe, and stay away from those that will ruin your E.M. building efforts, it's a good idea to understand typical behaviors that people have, and how they relate to their level of emotional intelligence. Which also relates to their level of healing, of how much trauma they have, and the efforts they are willing to invest. Some people will just keep using you as a pressure valve for the stuff they can't deal with within themselves. There are plenty of people who know very well that they are mean and hurtful to others, and they don't care much, stay away from them, really. They can be entertaining, but so can a house full of spitting cobras, unless you're standing right in the middle of them while trying to play the castañuelas. I'm convinced some of you relate to this, and might have even cracked a smile on that one:)

Again, it is not to completely avoid people that are not super high in E.M., but to find people that are **complimentary to your journey**. Like if you have problems managing your finances, and you meet someone who's awesome at budgeting, but they tend to get depressed sometimes, and you are always cheerful, that is complimentary, not perfect people, but a good match. But some people aggravate their lower points, and belittle their strengths, like someone teasing you because you are so good at keeping your house clean, because they are not happy about their own difficulties with that, that is not complimentary, they work against your strengths, trying to make themselves feel good about their own weakness. Or two guys that can't deal with their emotions in a healthy manner, and instead of encouraging each other to go to a therapist, to exercise, or take a vacation, they keep going to the local pub to drink, they aggravate their weaker areas and keep themselves from growth.

To keep making progress to that awesome life, you need to keep things like that in the back of your mind, the ways the people in your current social groups interact with each other, and with you, how you feel with them, if you feel uplifted, or always defensive and depleted. Complimentary people and environmental conditions can "make it or break it" in regards to getting to your true potential.

Here is a basic list of things to look out for, to assess, not only in others, but in you as well. To know what you can work on, to figure out how complimentary you can be for others, and others with you. I have mostly avoided repeating the opposites, but you can factor that in, like I do mention that people with high E.M. are mostly honest, and people with low E.M. tend to lie, but I have avoided many other opposites or tried to turn them a bit, even though they apply.

People with high E.M. tend to:

- Be consistent
- Apologize for their mistakes, owning up to them instead of blaming or deflecting
- Not engage in drama
- Are honest and authentic
- Loving and compassionate
- Not prone to over-reacting
- Will consider your needs and feelings
- Are willing, and able, to compromise in a fair manner
- Will not ridicule or disparage you if you make a mistake
- They can be serious, but they don't take themselves too seriously
- Know their boundaries and limits

- Do what they can to help people improve their situation, without over-extending themselves

People with low E.M. tend to:

- Make excuses for pretty much anything, and not apologize
- Get offended very easily
- Use sarcasm and teasing often, and be very mean with it
- Laugh *at* people, not *with* people
- Lie a lot, even those white lies they like to dismiss as for "the benefit" of the recipient
- Procrastinate
- Generally driven by fear and selfish motives
- Often talk/think in negatives (Could be better, not enough, I hate this or that, bad things always happen to me)
- Explosive/exaggerated behaviors and expression
- Monopolize conversations, interrupt often
- Will often change the subject when you try to talk about meaningful, emotional topics
- Will not want to reflect on the past, for going through the painful moments, to get over stuff
- Become envious, jealous, angry, resentful, at anyone else's success
- Don't handle change very well
- Are happy when you fail, or when you get hurt

Not a complete list of course, but enough to give you a good start.

*People that are not "perfectly" complimentary, that sometimes aggravate some of your trauma and conditioning can be helpful to you, and possibly indispensable on your journey, they can be your greatest teachers. So being fully complimentary is not *all* about peace and love and candies and flowers. We do need people and situations to trigger our pain now and then, as long as it is not always, and remains within our capacity to cope with in a healthy way. By bringing those things to the surface, we can then deal with them properly, as they get pulled out of the depths of our subconscious. If they always remain hidden to us, there is nothing we can do to get over those things. So a healthy balance is required, and the more loving your whole environment, the easier it will be to heal from those things when they get triggered into the present moment.

Developing a New Vocabulary

I've put this here because of the importance it has in interacting not only with yourself, all your parts, but with other people as well, so it will help you in finding your tribe, your place in this world, knowing who you can be "you" with. It is a very important topic, to know who you are, to get all of your parts communicating the proper messages between them, the proper feelings, to heal at a deeper level, and to prevent further abuse and trauma from being improperly integrated in your system.

Think of this example: A new term I have been hearing recently, called "***body-shaming***". This term and others like it is an example of people growing up emotionally, to be able to properly express feelings, and to know how to draw a line. Before this term, how many women (as mostly women use it now) have been made to feel all sorts of things by others because of their bodies, without really knowing how to express it, without having a word to put on the pain they felt, or say anything about it. Yes, even looks can be abusive, stares, judgments, negative comparisons. We need to understand what abuse is, how abuse and trauma get/got stored in our system, and how to express ourselves better, to reconcile all of it.

So, developing a better emotional vocabulary to express our feelings, our experiences, and have the courage to explore our imperfections. But it is not just a vocabulary of words, not like learning Spanish, it is a **whole body communication system of sorts**, to get all of your parts speaking the same language. Yes it can include words, but not just words, it is linked to your emotions, your memories, your trauma, your dreams, your desires, your past, and your present, all of you. Think of the term "body-shaming", it is not just a word or expression, it is about not letting people make you feel bad about yourself, to be comfortable with who you are, to draw the line, to express hurt, but strength also, resilience. All of your parts communicating the same thing, knowing, feeling, expressing, to a greater purpose.

When we don't understand our feelings, they get stuck in our system, as our system doesn't know what to do with those feelings, as happens so often in childhood. Again, so much trauma starts there. When children are introduced to emotions they don't understand, or not allowed to express, all those emotions can get stuck within them, causing trauma. All those fears, wounds, pains of all sorts, swirling around endlessly until they can be freed from their timeless prisons.

Back to the example: If a woman does not have an understanding of the pain someone might cause her, let's say a "dirty look" she gets from a co-worker because of her appearance, that pain will simmer inside of her, will often become anger, or, yes, shame for how she looks. She can feel the pain of it, but if she cannot properly make sense of it, to give it a name, to say no to it, then it will stay inside of her. But if she gives it a name, understands what it is, and how it makes her feel, to say I don't like to be "body-shamed", I will put an end to it, I will tell people that "body-shaming" makes me feel bad about myself, keep your "body-shaming" to yourself. Then, oh, well, a completely different story. The dirty look might still cause pain, but that pain follows a healthy course, as the person can now act like a lightning rod to it, because they see it, understand it, and are able to let go, or direct it back to the sender. They will most likely not carry it further, it will most likely not contribute to their dysfunctional matrices, and the person not only becomes a model to themselves, but to everyone else. We don't always need to invent new words for the stuff we must deal with, but the idea is to find the proper words to your feelings and emotions, to know where they come from, their relationship to your past, and to your present, and recondition them to healthy outcomes. The pain of how women have been treated for their bodies has been known for a long time, but sometimes giving a known source of suffering a new term that makes more sense can help to overcome that pain for everyone.

"The best gift you are ever going to give someone; the permission to feel safe in their own skin. To feel worthy. To feel like they are enough..." – **Hannah Brencher**

If that doesn't summon up some courage to stand up to those abusive people, mean words and ill intents, well, read on... (Well, read on anyway, cause, you know, you've gotten this far, why stop now)

Expect this emotional vocabulary thing to develop in the coming years. It'll help people reclaim their power not only from abuse and trauma of the past, but from the people who would take advantage of them in the present. Many people use their emotional heft to control and subjugate others around them, knowing that some are just not strong enough emotionally to tell them off, to stand up for themselves... As any growing vocabulary, it isn't perfect, and sometimes we might need to push harder as we explore it, but that's part of the learning curve we should allow ourselves.

We need to grow the courage and talk out our emotions and feelings. If someone gives themselves the right to shame you (or any other form of abuse), **then why not give yourself the right to call them on it?** Are you jealous because I am thin, or voluptuous? Do my talents threaten you? Are you angry for my sense of style, what is it that I have that bothers you? Nothing, then why are you attacking me in that way, why do you talk about me behind my back? It's either out of love, anger, or jealousy, which is it? If it was nothing, you wouldn't bother...

*Check out this great poem, a grand lesson on emotional intelligence: *Still I Rise*, by **Maya Angelou**

Our society is becoming ill for the lack of emotional awareness, part of it is that we keep repressing more and more our feelings, and making excuses for it. By labeling it not polite, or not politically correct, or that it might be rude or this or that. But we all lose in the balance, except those who don't care, who can't love, they just come over and sweep up all the spoils, they torment and manipulate people to their advantage, and most people just keep repressing themselves a little more in the process.

The squeaky wheel gets the grease no more, the days of the role playing victims, complainers, and narcissists are over, let us all express what we need to express, and learn to reconcile our inner differences. If we don't talk, if we don't develop the vocabulary, then it is just a whole bunch of pain ping-ponging in between people, unresolved issues, your pain to my pain, my pain to yours, back and forth. No healing, it just gets worse.

More on developing this new vocabulary in the journaling section.

Attuning and Bonding

The deepest desires that we have relate to bonding to others in a healthy way, that is why the fear of rejection can be the worse feeling to have, even more than the fear of death. All of those anti-social traits from the Dark Triads, they all work against the bonds people try to develop and maintain with one another. Some members of those dark triads form bonds within their groups, through violence, terrorism, misery of all sorts, subversive activities and addictions, and so forth. But those bonds destroy life, they don't create it, which is why those people always seek ways to harm, rather than to uplift, to separate the whole from one another, rather than to unite humanity to greater good.

Love is the desire to bond, to feel the healthy connections of our energies meshing together, dancing, smiling, dreaming... It is a deeply soothing feeling, like returning to our mother's womb, nurturing, healthy companionship. Careers, entertainment, activities, are all means to that end, not the end unto itself. That is why many enlightened people have mentioned something about us returning to the great ocean, where we all become one again. That is what we seek through our notions of love, for our connections to be so strong, as to feel as if we are all drops of the ocean blending into one another. But so many things hinder that healthy bond, that disrupt our energetic connections and keep us isolated.

Unconditional love is an idea, romantic suppers are simply means, behind all of that is a desire to bond, to feel a person, our energies to theirs. The most satisfying bonds are those that have the least amount of baggage between the connections we try to create, again, emotional maturity can take us there. The more people follow that path, the less we have to worry about what the world will become, things will just keep on getting better and better.

This might very well be what human beings seek the most out of their existence!

Again, attuning yourself to complimentary people, not perfect, but complimentary, not only in regards to finding your tribe and developing higher E.M., but to allow a much deeper connection with fellow humans, that nurturing connection, which might be what love is all about when you think about it. Again, by complimentary, I don't mean always smooth sailing, never any arguments, what certain people think should be the ideal match. If the things inside of you that need to be healed never get triggered, then your chances of healing them will be practically nil. In a complimentary relationship, there is still conflict, but the conflicts become opportunities for growth, instead of merely acerbating the issues that cause the conflict within yourselves, and in the relationship.

Also, again, keep in mind that our systems naturally bond with the people we spend most time with, our energies mesh with theirs. On the surface, it might not sound like such a bad thing, but consider that for the people you have bonded with, those energetic attachments, by carrying them, you also carry some of their wounds, their trauma, all the stuff they have not managed to heal. The attachments, the bonds, they are energetic, and they link you to others, the good and the bad. So when you struggle to make your life better, you not only struggle against your own fears and issues, you struggle against those of the people you have bonded with.

As no one is perfect, we must accept that part of life, but as we try to progress, to make our lives better, that is a very important factor to consider in regards to keeping with complimentary people, otherwise the connections you make with others can greatly impede your progress, and even make you fall behind, far behind. Also, if we are not mindful, we can also create unhealthy bonds with our possessions, many develop emotional attachments to their houses, cars, clothes...

All the things we own can end up owning us, something to be careful about.

Rescuing your Lost Selves

Taking a few steps back from developing your emotional vocabulary and healing your dysfunctional emotional matrix, considering all those parts of you left to wander the dark forests of your subconscious, this is another way you can explore your inner self. To look at all of "you" with those brand spanking new E-Glasses you've been working on, well, not actually new, a bit cleaner, not so dysfunctional, and preferably without spanking either, well, hmm, let's just stick with renewed...

Soooo, once you start getting a better idea of the lay of your land, you, the people around you, an improved grasp on your emotions and feelings, and an environment that can support your own exploration. You might start to feel stuff stirring deep within you, things that are now trying to get your attention. Those feelings might feel good, but they can also feel scary, unwanted. We have a lot of our lost parts, our trauma, that feels unwanted or unloved, and to face their suffering might also make *us* feel unwanted, or shameful, bruised, abandoned, but we *must* face those feelings, that is a process of growth we cannot avoid.

Re-associating the right Emotions to your Experiences

Those stuck experiences and emotions I have been talking about that create your dysfunctional matrices, Ego and Ega, well, think of those things that are stuck as parts of who *you* were then. Parts of your self that could not deal with the situations they found themselves in in a healthy way, then became fractured off, isolated from the whole. Like an actual part of your personality, part of "you" that gets stuck in the past, alongside the emotional trauma. Like I have said, every bit of trauma has a mind and emotion component to it, masculine and feminine, Ego and Ega, and that mind component is a sort of "mini-you", a snapshot of who you were then, and you can say that a part of you gets stuck in the emotional system as well.

And since those parts of you were not able to deal with the emotions of an experience, let's say your father yelling at you as if you had just committed a murder, even though you only broke a glass. Then that part of you will be stuck facing the emotions it wasn't able to face in perpetuity, until it is healed and let go of, reclaimed. That poor little you, at 8 years old on a cold November day, dropping a glass by accident, and so afraid of your father's wrath, that a part of you, the most fragile and innocent part, broke off from the whole and ran into the dark abysses of your mind's subconscious, which became part of your Ego, and the emotions it could not face got stuck in your pain body. That is why you must understand all of those parts of you that are stuck in your Ego, in the past, and their associated stuck emotions in the Ega, **and find a way to reconcile their "broken" relationship**. Like in the example, as long as you don't find the courage to face and heal the fears of your little 8 year old self that got lost, it will remain as part of your Dysfunctional Mind Matrix, a part of your Ego, and Ega, that will most likely sabotage you in many ways. It could develop passive aggressive behaviors, problems with authority, become a perfectionist and scared of messing up anything, or might just stay there, sulking in a corner, and making you lazy and afraid of change. So imagine all kinds of parts of you in similar situations, all pulling you in various directions, creating problems in relationships, at work, with your own children, all keeping you from your dream life.

Those hurtful words from your father will keep tormenting that part of you, always, until you find that little 8 year old, confront the pain it is still being subjected to, to face the anger and rage of your father for the sake of that 8 year old version of you, and if successful, you free that part of you from its prison of the past, and reclaim it into your present.

That is healing, that is emotional growth, and that is how we become more present and loving my friends...

MUSICAL INTERLUDE: I think it is a great time for this one; *Free*, by **Rudimental** and featuring **Emeli Sandé** (check out the official video!)

IMPORTANT NOTE: And to think that all of those dissociated parts stuck in the past, in trauma, in shame, blame, regrets, even memories you yearn to get back to, they all have a very slippery grasp on reality, if at all. They often don't communicate with one another, again, why it makes being present more difficult, and also decreases your ability to come up with a better plan for your life, and stick to it. To convince, to move *"all of you"*, all of those parts with so many different issues towards one great unified goal becomes very arduous, pretty much impossible. So the more you have unhealed stuff, the more errors in your buffers, the more separations in between various parts of your psyche. So you become more prone to disease and illnesses, emotional upsets and breakdowns, your capacity to think and focus decreases, and your ability to make healthy long term goals decreases as well. Then your life starts going around in circles, you don't move forward to great heights, it feels like you have so many different ideas, different desires that don't match up very well, you can't figure out what you could be passionate about, what a life of meaning would even look to you, let alone actually take steps towards it. To love, to be deeply happy, compassionate, and for our life to have meaning, we need to be whole to a greater extent within ourselves.

"Instead of resisting any emotion, the best way to dispel it is to enter it fully, embrace it and see through your resistance..."
– Deepak Chopra

You need to have all your parts on board, communicating, collaborating, to achieve greatness. Now, you can see in the world at large that there are not many people who have achieved such a feat, but there is no reason why *you* can't, and there is no reason why we can't increase the amount of people that strive, and achieve, greatness. We just need to understand the process a bit better, and do something about it. Again, that is why healing, developing deeper self-love, to get all those parts of you together deciding as a whole what your purpose in life could be, is the way to go.

And all of those repressed feelings, the stuff stuck there, they will all keep feeling exactly the same as they did when you experienced those things, the fear of that bully, whatever your mother and father did or didn't do, the freezing terror for being called out by your teacher... **You will need to feel all of that over again**, but in a loving way as much as you can, with the new strength and courage you didn't have back then, the one you are building up right now. Without building strength today, how can you be strong for those parts stuck in the past?

So, how *do* we confront the stuck emotions of the past?

Well, of course there is regular therapy, reading books like this one and some that are more specifically into healing or psychology, workshops, support groups... Discussing with the people in question, talking out loud on your own, to other people that are supportive. For the prior example, talking out the event with your father, or when alone at home, saying how mean it was, as it was just a glass, and how afraid it made you of him, how terrified you became of breaking anything else, how it created perfectionism, how it made you fear "screwing up", or simply forgive if you are able to... Speak out the words and the feelings that make sense not only to you, but to that 8 year old version of yourself. Be the voice, the strength, that it needed to have then. And you might have noticed, this is a similar idea to the other section about re-writing our past, but it is more specific to your trauma from childhood, and how to perceive your fractured selves as real as you are now, little parts of you fragmented into the exact situations they were not able to cope with, that caused them to run away from reality and get lost in the dark forests of your being. Just like a child running away from home into an actual forest, and losing their way, getting lost, afraid of animals, afraid of the night, of all kinds of sounds, creaking branches, the wind...

Think of all that childhood trauma, all the times when you needed a hug, when you faced the imperfections of your life, your school teachers, all the times you "checked out" of the present moment, when your mother or father were abusing you, yelling at you, scowling in such a way to feel they could kill you, or made you feel unwanted. Even being smothered in "love", and not able to deal with the attention, to be conditioned into over-achieving, pushed to succeed beyond what a child can bear... All those times when parts of you had enough of what was going on regardless of how good or bad the situation might appear, and just left the building, into the dark corners of your mind, of your body, into fantasy, day dreams, invented realities... All those situations, as a child or adult, can contribute to you becoming *less you* as life went by.

Our lost Children

To see those "lost parts" as mini-versions of you, from the exact moment they got lost, fragmented off into time and space, outside your timeline, well, think of this:

Why are many adults so emotionally immature? Why are adults not all emotionally mature, loving and responsible? Our bodies keep developing and "growing" up, how come some adults are very mature inside, and others are far from it?

Because a lot of their trauma, their lost selves, comes *from* childhood. So their inner landscape is populated by their own selves, as children, running around in there, in fear, in pain, crying, wanting to be seen and heard, afraid of being beaten... All contributing to them behaving like children anytime something triggers those pains and trauma. Makes sense? I think so...

Why do adults often behave like children, spoiled, hurt, afraid of speaking their mind, afraid of authority, afraid of not making friends, feeling they are not good enough, afraid of being rejected, needing attention, hiding their pain, embarrassed to cry, afraid to fail, not accepting their adult responsibilities (bills, chores, parenting), and the list goes on, if they are in fact "fully" adults. Shouldn't adults behave like adults all of the time if they are "adults" through and through?

It is not too hard to make those connections, of the many dysfunctional ways adults can behave, to what children go through with their parents, at school, with siblings. Why would an adult be afraid of talking about their feelings? Why should they still need to prove who they are, that they are trustworthy, to not be afraid of losing friends, or of what people think of how they dress. Doesn't that seem like a ridiculous way for a "mature" adult to behave and act?

SIDE NOTE: I know I might say a lot of stuff that is a bit out there, some mind exercises and such, but I don't expect you to connect to everything that I talk about, as long as you get some good stuff out of it, to create a few cracks in your armor, that is enough for me, and it should be enough for you. Making true progress towards emotional maturity and healing is not so easy, so we should celebrate any progress, big or small. As many times the tried and true techniques can fall short of helping us in greater progress, then daring to tread off the beaten path becomes our only viable option, and in that, some divergences should be expected.

When you take enough time to look at your behavior, and the behavior of those around you, it is not so hard to start seeing the truth of this, in how many ways adults do indeed behave like children, very immature. From the way they dress sometimes, wanting the best "toys", the most friends, how they behave and act in certain ways just to belong, isn't that all childish in a way?

Taking the example of the pain body, the Ega, again think of it as being made up from all the pain that we have not managed to reconcile, to heal. It is made up of the pains from bullying, from not receiving attention, from being called a liar when you told the truth (or called out on your lies), from being abused, from being scared of the dark but your parents insisting you turn off the lights, from your physical hurts not gotten over with, not being taken seriously, not getting enough hugs and kisses. Those all create various forms of trauma, many of them distinct from one another. Separate parts within a whole, but still all interconnected. Being bullied by the biggest kid in school created a part of you that is afraid of bigger people perhaps. Maybe being tormented because you have red hair made you self-conscious about that part of you. Every time that bully bullied you, every time the last bell rang in school, the fears crept up of being beaten on your way home, every single time you experienced emotions that you were not able to manage, that part of you "checked out" from the whole, and ran away into your darkness, the closet of your being, and became a part of your Ega/Ego. Making you lash out at people that act like bullies, making you lash out at anyone who would judge your appearance, or cower and remain oppressed, the repercussions are great and varied. Even the fear of bells in the case of the bully, as it meant facing the walk home alone, and the fear of being preyed upon.

Again, you need to grow the courage to face the pains of your "lost children", to face the bullies, to become your own ideal parent, to let your inner children out to play all the games they were not allowed, or didn't have enough of, to love, to laugh, and, well, you get the picture. And they are all waiting, looking up to you to make it happen. If you connect to this, and want to do more "inner child" work, check out Matt Kahn's *letter to the inner child* for starters.

So, no more "children should be seen, not heard" emotionally immature crap from dysfunctional adults! You make your own rules from now on...

"I believe that this neglected, wounded, inner child of the past is the major source of human misery..." – **John Bradshaw**

When you start playing along, to not remain afraid of those dark things inside of you, to know they are all versions of you, pains of the past, fears, unprocessed stuff, then you can actually start to trigger those things on purpose, to help retrieve the dissociated parts, to let go of the barriers, and to help bring them back together, all of you as close to oneness as humanly possible.

So the inner child thing, it's good to keep in mind in regards to how you can speak to yourself at times, to notice behaviors that might feel child-like, or makes you think of actual experiences from your childhood, to speak in soothing and nurturing words and feelings, as if you are actually speaking to a child, your own, to enjoy, to overcome, to heal... Try it out, see how it goes!

Maybe we will never become *fully* adults, maybe parts of us will remain as children forever, and that might not be such a bad thing. As long as our "child-like" behaviors are not dysfunctional, but instead maintain an innocence and an appreciation of the simple things in life, that might be the way to go in our spiritual and emotional growth, another idea I'm throwing out there...

Also, in regards to those "lost parts". There is a popular system in psychology called **Internal Family Systems**, or *IFS*, that is similar to what I talk about here. To understand that we are not whole, that our various internal selves can be seen as one big family, and not just as children, but all sorts of archetypal characters. This model can be used to treat people much more effectively than regular psychotherapy, something you might want to check out.

From the official website/institute: *"Internal Family Systems is a powerfully transformative, evidence-based model of psychotherapy. We believe the mind is naturally multiple and that is a good thing. Our inner parts contain valuable qualities and our core Self knows how to heal, allowing us to become integrated and whole. In IFS all parts are welcome.*

IFS is a movement. A new, empowering paradigm for understanding and harmonizing the mind and, thereby, larger human systems. One that can help people heal and helps the world become a more compassionate place."

Though I have put more emphasis on healing and *incorporating* our fractured parts, understand that we can never do this fully, some of those parts will always remain as parts of the whole. The idea is to heal as much as possible, and for the parts that remain separate, to have them all on board towards a greater destiny. So when we say our deepest wounds can become our best gifts when healed, I believe it has something to do with this. Our deepest wounds create the biggest separations within us, and when we heal those fractured selves from their "deepest" wounds, they can become our strongest, most fearless allies, for the strength they have gained and the trust and love we have built with them going through the pain they/we were carrying.

Building back Trust

So building back trust with those parts, making them feel wanted and loved, and safe enough to have faith that those bad experiences are over, and that the present is a much better place to live in. Which means not having abusive people in your current environment that trigger them back into hiding or into their fears, for your life to be more supportive of love and compassion, nurturing and soothing, isn't that like what I've been talking about? Self-love, finding your tribe, developing in E.M. to better care for *all* of yourself, and taking the time to build a very healthy environment and habits...

That the "you" that went on living is now an adult and can make better decisions, to remove any person that is scary to them out of your life, that you can face any fear they were not able to face back then... As mentioned earlier, that is part of re-parenting ourselves, a great part of the healing process and a powerful tool to add in your arsenal.

"As a matter of fact I had a terribly traumatic childhood. But afterward I sort of reraised myself..." – **Michael Gruber**

Of course trauma is not all about childhood, there's a lot of stuff that happens to us in adulthood as well. And as you get into it, you are bound to start getting some flashbacks, feelings and memories from long ago, sometimes at the conscious level, other times as vague feelings. Again, check out the works of *Pete Walker* in regards to emotional flashbacks, how they happen, and how they can give you a clue as to where they come from, meaning what kind of trauma/wounds could be responsible for them, and that can give you an idea of what to address, to heal those parts.

Keep in mind the "being kind to yourself" thing, always. There is great learning in our mistakes, drop the perfectionism, it's a terrible vestige of a dysfunctional childhood and often keeps us locked in very unhealthy patterns of aching to live up to our parent's expectations, and avoiding making any kind of mistakes. Which means always sticking to the tried and true, and never growing out of our emotional childhood. Break a few things, yell out, dare to be heard talking to yourself in public, cry, call someone out on their hurtful behavior at the risk of misinterpreting the situation!

So please, win those parts of you back into the present, learn about them, earn their trust, love them back into your life. Let them know that *now* is a better place to be in, that you can better protect them, to keep them safe and feeling loved for all the love they missed out on...

Being Your Own Role Model

If you take all of this seriously, if you don't allow yourself to give up, to get discouraged, but not to get obsessed either, doesn't this all come together to feel as if you are becoming your own model to follow?

What greater life can you have than to be your own role model? Yourself, being the image of the person you can look up to, that you can hope to be one day. But that day is now, in the present. You have lived up to your dreams, your life as a love letter to yourself, becoming your own version of a human being that you value and hold in high esteem. Not perfect, not ideal, with room to grow, **but in the process of growing in all the right ways**. You have found your own path, your feet match the grooves in the sand, you are at peace with your place in this world, romantic relationship or not, tons of friends, or not even one close enough to call a best friend, it's okay, you know you'll make it, you *are* making it. Because again, those goals are not the end of the world, and deep down, you know it, you feel it, you *are* "it". It isn't a place, the conditions of your environment count for something, but they don't define you, that sense of belonging is within you, the person you look up to is now *you*. There are still some people out there you look up to as well, but only as a "refining" process to your own self, not something you ache for that is outside, or for the kind of life you *wished* you had, but only as extra elements that could help, but are not necessary.

You get knocked down, you get up, you notice some areas where you struggle, you seek help and you know who to ask, and how. You don't need drugs or alcohol or other unhealthy habits to make it through tough times, because you have learned how to manage, you have built up enough strength to know you'll get through it, and you know who you can trust with your feelings, and who you can't. All contributing to an increased presence, awareness, sense of self.

Just like a marble statue, little chips here and there can help to create a masterpiece when the tools are held by capable hands, and eyes that have a vision of the masterpiece in the making. You start shining, people start noticing, some are happy for you, and some are jealous, and for those jealous ones, well, you will need to learn how to avoid them, and how to protect your shine if you can't. So the journey isn't over, it might never be, but the destination doesn't seem so important anymore.

"Your trials did not come to punish you, but to awaken you –
to make you realize that you are a part of Spirit and that just
behind the sparks of your life is the Flame of Infinity..."
– Paramahansa Yogananda

And think about this for a while: If you are *not* your own role model, what does that mean to you, how does it make you feel, that you are not the role model of your own life? How far away from it do you think you are?

Being there for yourself in ways that you need someone to be there for you, we usually don't think of us in that way, but who else to play that role above all others?

To not only heal all of your parts, but to become the leader, to have them as your trusted board of directors, listening to you because you have earned their trust, you have managed to free them of their pain, and brought them to order as a unit waiting for your commands. In peace and harmony, not only with your full being, but in harmony with your life, with your reality, with what you do, and with what you don't do, and with others as well. Always the best decisions, always the shortest path to any goal you create for yourself.

Wow, such idealism, such grandness, what can I possibly add to that!?

But I think, well, I know, that we're not there yet, not only individually, but as a whole.

To continue the endeavor, how about we learn how to protect our borders from enemy incursions and unhealthy energy exchanges?

Developing Intelligent Boundaries

Developing intelligent boundaries works hand in hand with assessing your environment and making healthy changes to it, but it goes a few steps beyond. Think of it as an ***advanced personal active defense system*** combined with an increased ability to express yourself fully, as you are, and reap all the treasures that love and compassion can bring into your life.

Vulnerability is difficult, and without it, emotional maturity is very difficult to increase and true love remains elusive. If you do not build up proper healthy boundaries, you will struggle greatly to allow yourself to be vulnerable without fears of future pain, let downs, people taking advantage of you and such. Which is obvious really when you think of it, and quite understandable.

Who wants to be vulnerable when their history has shown them how painful it can be?

Most people have heard about "normal" boundaries, but just like with "normal" E.Q., normal boundaries can leave us with too many weak spots, or walls too thick to let anything or anyone in, our out. Whereas ***Intelligent*** Boundaries are strong and alert defenses that can allow the good stuff to come in, block the bad, and permit healthy vulnerability without the weaknesses of the bleeding heart seeking to be loved at all costs. That is the only path to unconditional love, to heal old wounds and trauma, to greater abilities in emotional maturity. **The best of relationships require people to have intelligent boundaries**, otherwise those relationships will always be the kind that many people get stuck in, you open yourself up for a while, you get hurt, you close yourself up for a while, you get resentful and lonely, you try again. Next time it seems different, until it becomes apparent that it is not, you close yourself off again...

You know the drill, a bit like a psychotic clam opening up and exposing all the tender parts, then the slightest movement triggers it into closing off into a hard shell, open again, close, open, close...

"Daring to set boundaries is about having the courage to love ourselves even when we risk disappointing others..."
– Brené Brown

With intelligent boundaries, those dysfunctional patterns become a thing of the past. You can sense the people that you just can't trust, and you keep your energies closed off to their attacks, their intrusions, but without closing yourself off to the people you *can* trust, and you get to learn the difference. It's not an "all or nothing, completely closed, or completely opened" kind of thing. You have multiple levels, dynamic, you can be at a party, and switch your defense strategy on the fly, depending on who you are interacting with, ain't that the sweetest thing?

A narcissist comes along while you are engaged in talking to someone you care about, and you can have an energetically "closed" interaction with the narcissist, while maintaining your good humor with the person of interest. All flowing seamlessly without a hitch. No more blowing up, thinking that damn whoever ruined your chances, they "made" you so mad, and believing you can't allow your defenses to be down ever again, not wanting to compromise your chances with people of interest, at the cost of the narcissists/ill intended people invading your energy.

Considering that narcissists and people with dark personalities are very attracted to the good energy levels of people that take the time to heal and make themselves more positive, you can understand the importance of protecting that extra shine from them. They'll come and try to rub some of that off sooner or later, either by trying to take you down a few notches, or find a way into your heart, to own it as a trophy on their mantle.

"No is a complete sentence..." – **Anne Lamont**

The tricky thing about increasing our E.M. and becoming more loving, is that we then value deeper relationships even more, so we want to share ourselves as we grow. So you'll want to be more open, you'll want to be more trusting and allow yourself to be vulnerable, so you *will need to learn* who you can be like that with, and who you simply cannot. And when in mixed company, best to be able to manage yourself in the most healthy way possible, to not close down, to not lose some of that progress, and still be able to bond with people that have chosen a similar path. And yes, **just saying no is completely acceptable**, no need to explain and make excuses. Sure you can talk about it if you wish, but if you just feel like answering no to someone who asks more than they should, intrudes in your space, or you feel their energy is unwelcomed for whatever reason, **just say no**. That is a healthy part of monitoring, and respecting, your energy levels and emotional boundaries.

Human beings want to bond with others, that is what adds great value to our existence, but ever since we have left our small communities to live in bigger towns and cities, it has put a great strain on some of our deeper needs. And also, our need to bond, and feel connected, puts an increased stress on our fears of rejection and abandonment, and also why it can be very difficult to say no. And when living such individual lives as we are now, who can we trust when almost everyone is a stranger to us? Even our small social circle, many of our friends and family members have their own social circles that are unknown to us, no intermingling, which can make bonding with them scary as well, as people have all sorts of backup plans if things get more complicated, or even more personal, than they can manage. Again, take it easy on yourselves, we do live in a complicated world that makes it very difficult to express our feelings, to bond, and grow from an emotional perspective.

The Energy Exchange, the most Important Market to keep an Eye on

Bonding with people that we know and trust is very soothing and comforting. Just like a mother bonds with her newborn child, they become attuned to one another as they both open themselves up to the experience with little barriers in between them. Just like a tuning fork when hit can make another tuning fork resonate. We are all beings of energies, frequencies, and we all resonate to our own unique vibrations, and seek to share that with others.

Again, the importance of properly choosing the people we spend our time with, to bond, to attune to frequencies that are a healthy match to us, and for us to be a healthy match for them also. The more we bond, the more we attune, the more our energies mix, the more we become like one another. When we attune to people, we become attached for better or for worse, our energies line up, the channels open, and the more we do this the more our connection becomes intimate, strong. Then those people become more comfortable to us, and the more we want to be in their company. And this goes even for abusive relationships, just like the famous example of kidnapped victims attuning/bonding with their kidnappers, then falling in love with them.

Having your boundaries open to the wrong people will lead you down a wrong path for you, whether you leave those boundaries open on purpose or not. So developing intelligent boundaries is a must as you grow, otherwise your progress will be limited. Without them, you will often get hurt, people will take advantage of your increased level of compassion, and you will deplete yourself into all sorts of external places you might not even know about.

"When we attune with others we allow our own internal state to shift, to come to resonate with the inner world of another..." – **Dr. Dan Siegel**

Again, attunement leads to attachment, which leads to familiarity. This is great when it is reciprocal and healthy, but not so great when the person you are allowing yourself to attune with is selfish, self-absorbed, and not at all interested in personal/emotional growth, or just simply not a good match for you.

So, best to know people before you allow yourself to bond with them, don't you think?

Otherwise you are opening your energy system to them, your heart, for them to do pretty much as they please. Keep in mind that energy often averages out to the lowest denominator, as people with very low E.M. are most likely not willing to compromise, to always demand, not give anything, and be very selfish and self-serving. So those with higher E.Q., or E.M., will often bend their way, as being the more "mature" and compromising. When you do this once in a while, fine, but making a habit of it will drain the heck out of you.

Don't dismiss the power that people have of influencing you from the inside once you have allowed yourself to bond with them, to attune to their energy, even if they are not physically around you, those connections transcend any distance. And even years later, if you have not done some work to create the separations they can keep on influencing you well past the expiration date of the actual relationship, as often seen with parent/child bonds, or with siblings, and ex's too! So exercise caution... Unfortunately many people are way more protective of their cars, or other possessions, than they are about their own beings, who they become intimate with, who they allow their energies to blend with. Isn't that weird when we think about it? So be cautious of who you "shack up" with, meaning anyone you open yourself to, energetically speaking, the doors you leave open to your inner "castle". Such a beautiful instrument when well tuned, but such disorder and chaos when not, be careful who you allow to fiddle with it.

"Man's unique agony as a species consists in his perpetual conflict between the desire to stand out and the need to blend in..." – **Sydney J Harris**

Developing intelligent boundaries is like building up your emotional immune system to guard yourself from all sorts of invading forces, emotional viruses, jealousy and greed and all sorts of other negative energies. And it is also about protecting your investment in yourself, increasing in emotional resilience, to rise up, to step outside of your house and say "This Is Me", and damn anyone of you who try to mess with that!

Guarding the Castle

As an exercise, consider yourself, your energetic being, as a house, no, a nice little castle. Not too fancy, but the more you grow in E.M., in confidence and strength, the more this little castle will be pleasant to you, to fulfill all of your wishes, and will start attracting the attention of others. As with any castle, it needs to be guarded, so it has a fence surrounding it, its own defense system, at least it should have.

When you have very low E.M./E.Q., your castle is kind of in disrepair, like an abandoned building, broken windows, no doors, attracting homeless people, drug users, rats, cockroaches, bad influences of all sorts. Your fence is damaged in many places, fallen trees breach the perimeter here and there... Some people have their front gate wide open, anyone can come in no matter how ill their intents, while others have them completely shut, barricaded, but regardless, the perimeter is open to invasion no matter how guarded they think they are. Developing Emotional Maturity, and Intelligent Boundaries, is to ensure the whole property is well guarded all around and in very good condition overall. A great place where people want to go to and feel invited, welcomed, and no one can come in without your knowledge, without your approval.

Your front gate is not a moat full of alligators, nor is it wide open and without any security, it is a healthy balance of the two. You can allow yourself some vulnerability, without being terrified of the cost of it. You can invite guests without needing all sorts of background checks, and you naturally filter the guest list to those that will not try to steal everything that is not bolted down. You know yourself, and you know what you can tolerate, what is not healthy, and where to draw the line on unwanted behavior. And you are not afraid to kick out those who cause trouble.

No one can just blindside you, to stay indefinitely, come in uninvited, pee in the pool, break things. Those kinds of guests, you have learned to sort out of your life. You can be more restful, you see situations as they are, as you only have a small section to be mindful of (the front gate), the rest takes care of itself. You don't need to always walk around your property all the time to check the damage, who might be coming in and all that, **your fences/defenses are active, intelligent, and they manage all of your systems**. Surrounding yourself with caring people only makes it easier.

That is living life with intelligent boundaries, high E.M., anyone coming to you with deceit, with anger, with lies, you can spot them a mile away, their energy feels off to you, their cursed "gifts" have a certain smell that alerts you to some kind of poison. And since you have spent a lot of time ridding yourself of your own pain, of your own poison, you are more sensitive to not allow that stuff back into your flourishing property.

Caring and compassionate people are consistent, you know what to expect from them, and they will not try to circumvent your defenses. So as soon as you feel something wrong, you will have a pretty good idea of who you are dealing with, so then you can raise your guard accordingly, to not allow yourself to attune to them, to befriend them, to not mix your energy. But you can still remain vulnerable to the other people in your surroundings that do not raise any alarms. That is having intelligent boundaries, to not completely shut off every time you feel that something is wrong just because one person might have triggered your defenses, your trauma, your pain... People with low E.M., that have a lot of unhealed trauma, often over-react to any such events that might trigger them. It is not their fault, they have experienced so much, but until they learn to free themselves of some of it, unfortunately their lives will be like that, either completely blocked, or completely open, both with unfortunate consequences.

Like with the news, they make a big deal of one person who did something bad, and then people with low E.M. start seeing bad everywhere they look, always on guard. Unfortunately that is a tool of subversion often used in societies, and how we end up giving our power away for free, or without much struggle, when we remain in low E.M. mode.

> "Your personal boundaries protect the inner core of your identity and your right to choices..."
> **– Gerard Manley Hopkins**

And in regards to defenses, be weary of those people that amuse themselves in testing them, trying to spot vulnerabilities in your defense shield, they might make it seem like a game, but often they are deceitful and just trying to find a way in, or to make you feel bad about yourself. The further you get along this path, and you start sharing what you are doing, you will most likely encounter some of those from time to time. Trying to prove you are not as "healed" as you claim you are, not as whole or emotionally mature, or not as impervious to attacks. Their attempts speak volumes to their intent, so act accordingly. And heck, while you're at it, if they allow themselves some liberties, maybe you can do the same, and practice drawing some lines in the sand, deep grooves that will help you to increase your courage, like calling out their behavior as hurtful and mean for one, in a nice, but firm way.

Developing intelligent boundaries can make your life so much more peaceful, your interactions with kind people will become more open and compassionate, not always worrying about big bad wolves coming to hurt you. And if they do come along, you know you can just send them packing. That cute little red hood will not work on you any longer, blind to the wolf in sheep's clothing act no more, and they won't be able to slither in unnoticed. You won't need to use your mind to assess their intent, you will feel it in your heart, no judgment, just a knowing. Again, seeing and feeling from the eyes of your heart, intelligent boundaries are a good part of it, to maintain your integral form against the storms, keeping your energy systems intact and fully functional.

FOOD FOR THOUGHT: Although it can seem like a lot of work at times, you can have fun with it. Like going at parties and social gatherings, even at work, thinking that you are going on a treasure hunt in the Amazon forest, looking for diamonds, or diamonds in the rough, while avoiding quick sand, sloths, snakes and scorpions. Learn to look at people for what they are conveying, their intent, the warmth of their smile, a glitter in their eyes, or do they seem like predators on the prowl seeking prey, or snakes looking for people to dig their fangs in just for the fun of it. You will learn how to tell them apart, maybe not completely, but enough...

Again, people are complicated, and to understand that we are all human, some days are better, some days are worse, sometimes we allow ourselves to be bad, knowingly or not, other times we can do greater things. So drawing the line is never an absolute "good or evil" kind of thing. You will need to judge for yourself where that line is for you, and then accept the choices you need to make to uphold it.

It all relates to assessing your environment in a healthy way, finding your tribe, making changes. Don't make too much of it though, as you grow in E.M. things will start to make sense, and it won't take so much energy to actively think about things. The intelligence of your being, your intuition and inner compass will start taking over some of the decision making process, and it will be more about following and trusting how you feel, and less about having to think about all the little details with your mind, which makes it overwork and crash, like the blue screen of death. (again, dating myself...)

Dreaming the Dream

For these next two short sections, they are kind of related to a bit of everything, and I wanted to address these topics before getting into the final parts. I am talking here about literal dreams, the kinds you have when you sleep, but I believe they are also related to all of your life. They are linked to your greater purpose, and also the key to making your dreams a part of your reality.

First, we *all* dream, every night, even those that don't remember having them (apart from a very minuscule percentage of people that have a disorder preventing them from dreaming). It is a normal part of being human, and how our systems process information and emotions, to integrate, to learn, and to connect to our greater reality.

"There are some people who live in a dream world, and there are some who face reality; and then there are those who turn one into the other..." – **Douglas H. Everett**

I'm keeping this section short not because I don't think it is important, in fact, I think this topic is much more important than we realize. Though our understanding of dreams is still very limited, and there is so much I would want to say, but I feel the time, and space, is not quite right to get into it more than these few words.

I have journaled a great deal on dreams, my dream journals span over 25 years and across some 15 book-length volumes. Still, it is an elusive thing, dreams, and we do not have developed much of an understanding of them even though we have known of their importance for thousands of years. Science is still trying to explore what they are, what they mean, but I don't know when we will have true answers worthy of a better understanding. I do think they relate a whole lot to our emotions, to our lost parts, to all the dissociated and fractured selves stuck outside of the present moment, waiting to be re-integrated into the whole. And maybe the dream world is a place where all dimensions and energies intersect, it is always there, it does not disappear when we become awake.

So to make your physical dreams come true, in a way you'll need to master your dream world as well, as it relates to who you are as a whole. I'm not saying you'll need to actively work in your dreams, but as you heal, **as you grow in E.M., your dream world will also change along with the changes you make in yourself**. Your waking life, and your dream life, will start to blend in, to become more the same. As your dream life is related more to your subconscious, to the Ego and Ega, then the more you lessen them, the more those two worlds will become similar to one another, less dysfunctions to keep your "worlds" apart, the dream becoming reality. Which is why I believe nightmares are a very big sign that something inside of you is not well at all, as the more nightmares a person has, the more they have some of their parts in very bad places.

Through dreams we can get to understand ourselves on a different level, in a more direct connection to our subconscious, our whole reality, our dysfunctional matrices, but it can by such a wily place to explore. So this is a small heads up for their significance in your life, and how they change as you grow. To try and understand what they are trying to tell you, to point you in the direction that is best for your healing journey, towards making your waking days into your own **living dream**.

But, apart from elaborating a bit on nightmares in the next section, I will leave it at that. Keep in mind the idea that dreams are very much related to your emotions and fractured parts, and everything in your past that has not been healed and let go of. And also how it all affects your present life, your dreams of tomorrow, who you are, and how much of your life is not as you would like it to be, less than optimal.

Nightmares

Nightmares are a pretty big warning signal from your subconscious, not to be dismissed or neglected. Either related to past stuff that really needs your attention, or present day situations that are very unhealthy for you, or even future plans that might be scaring the heck out of some members of your internal family.

Think of nightmares, which are often about scary things chasing you, or things you are afraid of. Well, to think of those things chasing you, as *you,* as some of your lost parts. Parts of you left in pain, fears that you don't want to face, they chase after you, the dreamer of your dreams. So what you run away from in your nightmares, unfortunately are often your lost parts that are just trying to get your attention (or the fears they themselves run away from). Those parts of you repressed for so long, they just want your love, to overcome the things they are afraid of, because they can't do it themselves.

Those fears, the terrors in your nightmares, you must understand that they do not leave you when you wake up. For the people that are all relieved that their nightmare is "over" when they wake up, and they just wish to never have them again, those are warnings, so pay great attention to what is going on in your life, what triggered your nightmares, and what they might be trying to make you become aware of.

And again, those that are relieved once they wake up from them, know this: Whatever is causing the nightmare **does not go away** when you wake up! Those parts of you will keep on being tormented from whatever it is they are trying to bring attention to you.

Those are the trauma, the shame, the blame, the jealousy, the anger, the things we try to hide from others, even from ourselves. The things we don't accept of ourselves, or the things that have happened to us, that energy is within you, those fears that are eating away at you from the inside out, part of you is screaming out for you to pay attention. Again, either from something in the past, or maybe a threat in your present, or possibly decisions which you are about to make that will lead you down a path full of misery. And those things continue to chase us in the day, they continue to affect us from within, causing all sorts of emotional, psychological and physical ailments. Our dream world is not simply created when we fall asleep, then vanishes once we awaken. It is always there, parts of us are always in that dream world, a place beyond time and space. And when we sleep we visit them, embody those personalities similar to how people with multiple personality disorder embody specific personalities when they are awake. So we can use that time to understand all of ourselves at a much deeper level.

"I have had dreams and I have had nightmares, but I have conquered my nightmares because of my dreams..."
– Jonas Salk

Again, I have done a lot of research into dreams, and I have increasing knowledge of how they work, but it is somewhat premature of me to go into more details, but at the very least, do not ignore your nightmares. There are some good books on dreams, but regrettably none that I have found have that many straight answers, but still some are helpful. I wish I had more understanding of them to be of greater help, maybe in the years to come...

So, nightmares are telling you there is something wrong, like the "check engine soon" light in your car, ignore them at your own risk. Consider seeking therapy if you do have nightmares, or at least find a compassionate and caring person to talk to about them.

And if you are interested in remembering more of your dreams, which I suggest, a good practice is to keep a dream journal beside your bed and write in it every morning. Maybe at first you might not have much to write about, maybe nothing at all, but if you keep up the habit, your dream recall will improve with time. All it takes is 5-10 minutes in the morning, and you can get to know yourself even better for those few extra efforts.

PART 2.2: Love, the Language of the Universe

"It's about the journey – mine and yours – and the lives we can touch, the legacy we can leave, and the world we can change for the better..." – **Tony Dungy**

Removing the barriers to love is communing with the very nature of the universe, the energies that created it, and sustains it...

So yeah, I hear you, this journey is not for the faint of the heart. It truly does separate the weak from the strong, the courageous from the not so courageous. Emotional immaturity has such a devastating toll on all of humanity, most of what we struggle against has to do with people's incapacities to overcome their inner suffering and animal like behaviors. To remove that, our world would blossom like a flower of such a beauty never beheld by the human eye.

We're a long way from that, but with your efforts, we might get there yet.

I have introduced a lot of food for thought so far, and these last sections will serve to consolidate some of those ideas, what you can get out of it most, the big picture kind of thing, and also provide some important tools for you to make it all happen. That greatest life, the love letter to yourself, those E-glasses, E.M., and even towards Emotional Wisdom, more along the lines of those that have become lighthouses for humanity, all can be had to those that are willing to travel the roads less taken. The further you want to go, the more dedication it will require, and the more sacrifices on your part. That is a personal journey everyone must decide on their own, for whatever reasons make sense to them.

While considering how much work, investment in yourself you are willing to undertake, remember that all of it is not just for you, but for everyone else as well. All of the stuff you have within you, the pain, the trauma, the greed, jealousy, regrets, all of it, not only does it affect you on a constant basis, but people are often powerless of passing that on to others around them, especially those that are closest, it can't be prevented. Either directly, such as anger, violence, abuse, or indirectly, such as absence, negative feelings, talking behind their backs, not allowing them their own expression, not being vulnerable or developing deeper bonds. Which is why it all relates to making this world of ours a better place to live in, we each have a part to play in making it happen.

The goal is to not just *have* dreams, but also have the ability to make them happen. Big dreams don't come to those that don't have the courage to face all of what goes on inside of them, and even then, they don't come all at once, as all those "overnight" successes will attest to. They come in little steps, small improvements, and if you fail to consider those small "wins" each as their own little dreams come true, small parts of the actual dream, then your big dreams will always be out of reach. And again, same goes with love, once we develop a deeper capacity for it, we cannot prevent ourselves from passing it on to others as well, it becomes us, and people benefit from it. Where comes the importance of becoming more loving in our emotional maturity, then we keep passing on the good stuff, instead of the bad.

Adult responsibilities are not just about getting a job and paying your bills, they are about caring for our future, what kind of place we create and leave behind, the thriving of our species. Growing into those responsibilities requires effort, compassion, and a lot of love, not only for ourselves, but for others. Otherwise we remain as children, navel gazing until death, until time has run out.

So an emotionally responsible adult looks at the bigger picture of things, not just what they need to survive, but to what part they play in the story; from participants in the audience eating popcorn and drinking pop, to the main characters on stage moving the story forward to a splendid ending.

How Changing Ourselves is Changing the World

"Personal transformation can and does have global effects. As we go, so goes the world, for the world is us. The revolution that will save the world is ultimately a personal one..."
– Marianne Williamson

Yes, it can be done, you, yeah you, you're the one I'm talking to!!!

You think you can't make it, you think whatever you do will never amount to anything, that your life will go unnoticed, that your efforts will not contribute to a greater design, but I am saying yes, yes they can, belief is important, but actions speak louder than words!

The only way to truly advance, to truly have the life you would like, your dream life, is to develop not only the ability to see the bigger picture of it, all the details and such, but also to gain the ability to "feel" the bigger picture, that is how the law of attraction works... So again, the great importance of developing E.M. in all that you do, is to *feel* what is going on, the truth of it all, inside of you, and outside. So the true gifts of E.Q., and E.M., are not about learning "techniques" that you can use on your employees and co-workers (or hot date), but to know yourself at a deeper level, to find balance by sorting through your wounds and trauma, **then living life more from intuition than intellect, from love rather than survival.** That is how we will move humanity from merely surviving, to thriving. Some might call this quest spiritual, others love, or moving towards a greater power, God, Divine Intelligence, no matter how you see it yourself, that is the future of humanity, the new era, it *must be* if we are to see a world without wars and conflicts.

"Our human quest is to survive; our spiritual quest is to unite..." – **Asa Don Brown**

And to understand that true love is associated with our higher motives, spiritual, not just with our basic needs. There is no love in survival, only ensuring food and shelter and a few other niceties along the way, but those niceties will always take second place to survival anytime our fears and animal instincts get triggered. Hoarding resources will come first, power, control, dominance, greed, they will always win out against thriving when people focus on the lower emotions, when they don't increase their E.M.. When people are in survival mode in very small communities, then life can be not so bad, caring for one another, reducing threats and such, as our ancestors did. But when in survival mode in cities and bigger communities, things don't turn out well at all, the individual quest takes precedence over the well-being of the whole.

How do we get There?

Our society is not only inching more towards narcissism with every passing day, it is actually promoting it...

So, if the whole world gets created by what we do, and if what we do is greatly influenced by our perceptions of the world, our desires, and if those perceptions and desires get tainted by all of our fears, trauma and conditioning, then it stands to reason that our world gets created by the collective fears and trauma of the whole population. So then, the only way to undo that, to change the world, is to change our perceptions, to heal, to overcome our inner struggles, and that is not only how we can change the world, by changing ourselves, **but it is the *only* way to achieve that change**. Nothing can ever change without people changing themselves first, wars, conflicts, pollution, hunger, abuse, human trafficking, we all share in the responsibility of how the world is, and how the world becomes. That is why this greater revolution is on a personal level first, from the transformation each person is willing to attempt, and the level of success of each one of us.

Many would like to remain blind to that truth, and I don't blame them, well, maybe sometimes, my bad... But we just can't afford to maintain that blindness any longer. There is a time to play in the sandbox like children, without care of how the food gets on our table or how the bills get paid, and then there is a time to grow up!

Humanity is reaching that stage, the need to go beyond being emotional children and to face the truth about what we do with our time, who we are, and what we are capable of. Our society is moving at too high a pace to remain frozen in the wounds of our past.

> *"When you are born in a world you don't fit in, it's because you were born to help create a new one..."* – **Unknown**

Yes, we can make a difference, a lot of people are aching for that, but there are also a lot of people who are afraid of that truth, they would prefer to keep their lives unfeathered with those responsibilities. It is not easy to enjoy a latte at your favorite coffee shop knowing that we can do much more with our time when we allow truth to sink into our being. That doesn't mean to stop doing things we enjoy, but we do need to find a better, less selfish, balance.

So putting it that way, of course your best life is also everyone else's...

If we want anything to change on our planet, if we want to be able to face further calamities and difficult times like the current pandemic with more caring and compassion, if we want to hope for a humanity without terrorism and poverty, we will need to develop a better understanding of love and how it relates to emotional maturity, and consider the individual impact each and everyone has on the whole. To encourage one another to seek a healing path, rather than simply accepting a cheap facsimile of love, not to remain in the dark ages any longer, prisoners of our dark personality traits. As the quote says, love unites, not just two people, but everything, everyone.

Is humanity united at the moment? Nope, and far from it, just sayin'

Trying to change anything in this world of ours without first increasing our capacity for true unconditional love is like trying to teach a five year old what it's like to have children of their own. It simply will not work, they don't have the capacity to process that kind of information, or to do much about it regardless, as the lessons will not run deep. It might appear at times that we are making progress, but the problems will always come back as soon as there is something else that comes along to pull people's attention away from what they started.

History has taught us this over and over again, those are the patterns of life that will continue as long as we don't change ourselves. Poverty, climate, government reforms, abuse, hunger, disease... All those problems will always persist as long as we don't develop a capacity to love ourselves at a deeper level. A person who truly loves themselves loves others to the same level, so racism and terrorism will just fade in the background, people will stop polluting, corruption will vanish, trying to control others will stop, all forms of crimes will be greatly reduced, that is how we change the world.

And for healing, to overcome your internal stuff, another incentive is to think of the ego as cancer to humanity, it works against our best interests, it works against love and compassion, against the health of the whole "organism", so I think it's an apt way of looking at it...

"You have given your mind an impossible task by asking it to manipulate the world in order to fix your personal inner problems. Your mind is not qualified for that job. Fire it, and let go of your inner problems instead..." – **Michael A Singer**

Yes, I do tend to poke often, but people tend to sleep through life, so best to get poked back into reality than to face a bunch of regrets and unfulfilled dreams when the time of death is near and there is no time left to change anything. Humanity is waiting for people to wake up and smell the inner pollution that is taking over our planet, so I'll just keep on poking along in the meantime!

Endless cycles, that's what we are stuck in as long as our systems are mostly "offline", or I should say endlessly trying to process all kinds of unreconciled things in our buffers, the Dysfunctional Emotional and Mind Matrices. Just as people who were abused when they were young, if they don't heal, they will most likely seek out similar types of abusive relationships in their adult life, that is how we are made. We don't consciously seek out abuse (though some do), but our system seeks to heal, and it will keep showing you the abuse, making you experience it over and over until you finally get it, and get over it. The same as humanity in general, **our collective humanity will keep serving us the same dish over and over until we decide we've had enough**, then work hard to get something else that tastes better to our palate. With unconditional love, once you start experiencing the beginnings of it, nothing less will ever satisfy you again, you will see the great potential of where it can lead.

People that can experience true love will start dedicating their lives to that cause, not only for themselves, but for others. That is an unmistakable aspect of someone who can truly love, how much time they dedicate to increasing the level of love on this planet, rather than just seeking their own comfort and well-being. The less a person is able to love, the more their entire lives will be about their own pleasure and satisfaction, or spending their time trying to put out the interminable internal fires in their systems. Accumulating personal wealth, personal career objectives, materialism, individualistic goals, that is how a person behaves who is incapable of greater love. As they cannot feel for others, not even for themselves actually, why bother enriching the lives of anyone else?

"When a person can't find a deep sense of meaning, they distract themselves with pleasure..." – **Viktor Frankl**

To get a new Lease on Life

All of this to say that with low E.M., so much of what happens in life can devastate us, and so much of life confines us to repressing our feelings and desires, and in doing so, we end up living very "small", inside of us, and outside. We don't take risks, we avoid challenges, we are blind to great opportunities, life becomes limited in so many ways. When you are so terrified at the thought of losing one of your children, then you will greatly limit their lives to only safe paths. When you think that you would not be able to overcome the death of your partner, you will cling to him/her in a very unhealthy way. Fear of death of ourselves or anyone else greatly diminishes our life experience, and fears of loss of any sorts as well.

"To love yourself right now, just as you are, is to give yourself heaven. Don't wait until you die. If you wait, you die now. If you love, you live now..." – **Alan Cohen**

Our true genuine expression is required to live a great life, but when we are always so afraid of expressing ourselves, when we repress so many things, when we don't heal our past, our "genuine" self is also repressed, so repressed it becomes unknown to us, like a stranger, or even like an intruder within our own being (that we can run away from in our nightmares). And when we start knocking at the doors that hold it captive within us, if it answers, the sight of it can scare us, all those lost parts so foreign to us, like invaders we are afraid to face.

To grow out of our emotional immaturity is to accept everyone's right to peace and happiness, it is to stop seeing our own needs as more important than anyone else's, it is to consider all those little details of our lives, and the bigger ones too, as to how they might add, or subtract, to other people's lives. It's funny in a way, most people want so much to find love, to be happy, comforted, to feel a sense of purpose for their contribution, yet understand very little of what that means, or how to go about it. When we truly have a desire to look at it beyond our own needs, it becomes quite clear. Yes, a life filled with meaning and purpose doesn't come cheap, in regards to the sacrifices to our Ego and old ways of life, but really, if you knew the extent of it, that in the end, you're trading in coal for gold, weight for weight, well, do the math.

Like the song *"Heaven is a place on Earth"*, well not yet, but it could be.

It all has to do with love, how much of it do you want? That is the real prize we are after, and unlike land and resources, it is unlimited.

I know we can make this work, I have faith. We have so much to gain, everything in life gets renewed to better flavors, simpler pleasures, more trust and honesty, to understand what we do, and why we do it. Instead of threats all around, we start seeing opportunities, regrets get replaced by gratitude, the fears for our future subside into present awareness and courage to see ourselves through obstacles. And of course, relationships with the other more than 7.5 billion people on this planet improves. Yes, we can even care for strangers, knowing we can't help everyone directly, but still, to hold at least a minimum of compassion for everyone else. That "care" for others has a big role to play in how things will turn out.

Deeper Connections with others Starts with a Deeper Connection with you

The connections we create within ourselves, and with other people, those are the real connections that our world gets created with, what makes it what it is. What determines the fate of humanity is not the countries we have carved out of the terrain, not shipping lanes nor high speed internet infrastructures, not even cultures and technology, but the health and strength of the connections uniting us all.

The quality of the connections we create with one another, those invisible energy links between us, they work together to build the world and sustain it. Create weak connections with your friends, neighbors, co-workers, and everything that we build will have the same weaknesses. Create strong connections, healthy and loving, then everything will get created with that same energy, it will become the "backbone" of our world.

And to create healthier connections with people, we must take the time to know their values, their morals, their dreams and aspirations, their life experiences, how they feel in various situations. And if we don't start with us first, to know ourselves inside and out, our efforts are bound to fail.

MUSICAL INTERLUDE: I think a bit of a break is in order. Convincing the masses of your deeper beliefs can be hard work at times, for everyone involved. See, I wasn't kidding when I said I would repeat some things, but don't worry, there's loads of new stuff coming up. Anyway, it's still good to take a pause

The Foundational Elements of Love

FORGIVE!

Now that's an awesome beginning to this next section!

If there is one thing that you can do to help yourself on this journey of self-love, of building up emotional maturity, it is to forgive. And not just "say" it, but to mean it, to *know* what it involves, to know what you are forgiving, and why. And that is easier said than done.

And to understand that the only way to truly forgive, deeply, is to do it with as much love and compassion as possible, and that requires emotional maturity. Yes, it is yet another one of those things that you need *one* for the *other* to work effectively. There is a certain amount of magic in the process once things get going, to make those unseen forces of the universe work in your favor, but initially, it is more pain and hard work than serendipity. Sometimes it can seem like trying to juggle 5 balls at a time, and as soon as you take your eyes off of one, you lose focus and everything comes crashing down, but with time, the efforts become more seamless.

> *"There is no love without forgiveness, and there is no forgiveness without love..."* – **Bryant H. McGill**

And not only is forgiveness essential, it is *"primordial"*, another French term to mean that it is utterly necessary (you might have clued in a bit by now to my mixed origins). So, of *first importance*, that it cannot be dismissed. And also, forgiveness might be that one thing that you have most control over. Not necessarily control over the outcome, but it is within your power to use it, you decide the steps you are willing to take, and the results are more predictable. Love is vague, so is compassion and gratitude, you can't really *do* much about them in such a direct way as with forgiveness, they come to you as you heal, as you grow. Yes, loving gestures are under your power, but the outcome is not so easily ascertained. But forgiveness is more directly under your influence, yet so many people choose not to forgive, as if holding a grudge is a statement of the pain someone has caused them, to make them suffer for it, like being entitled to their suffering. But that's like sleeping on a bed of nails hoping to cause pain to someone else, life doesn't work that way.

Also, if you don't know your past, and are mostly unaware of what goes on around you, the stuff you have experienced, then how can you forgive things you are not even aware of? And as forgiveness is an important part of the E.M. building process, even **"incontournable"** (I'll let you look that one up yourself), then again, to review all your past, even if you don't think there's much there to forgive, is a must. You *will* find things to forgive, that is certain.

Now, **to forgive is *not* to forget**, and it doesn't mean you allow anyone to keep hurting you, or to open yourself up to further relationships with whoever you forgive. Many people believe that forgiving is merely letting go, that is not the case. Forgive and forget should *never* have been put together, it makes people think that to forgive is to disregard anything they might have done, or what others have done to them, simple as that. That is *not* forgiveness. Those that would try to convince you to "just get over it" are not on your side, they just want you to dismiss their behavior without them even owning up to it, and are likely to keep engaging in it. They might use the idea of forgiveness in the same manner as forgetting, but again, that has nothing to do with forgiveness.

You forgive for *you* first and foremost.

You can forgive an abuser and at the same time tell them you can't accept them in your life any longer, and that is perfectly fine. You can do it in person, you can do it over the phone, by email, or even just by yourself, just for you. There are many ways you can choose to forgive other than directly to the person, you can pray, you can visit a cemetery if the person is deceased, you can hold a picture of them and intend on connecting to the feelings of what you need to forgive them for, talk it out with a therapist or a friend. The importance is to open yourself up to the pain they have caused you, in all its shapes and forms, to forgive, and to let go of the suffering that was attached to the memories, to free them from your D.E.M..

But be careful not to forgive prematurely, or to offer a blanket statement such as "I forgive you" just to get it over with. It must be sincere, and you must try and **feel everything that is related to what you need to forgive** as much as possible, which is sometimes very difficult. And mention *what* you are offering the forgiveness for, be precise about it. Take for instance the physical abuse of a parent, and how much pain and suffering it caused you in your early years, how much joy it took away from an innocent childhood, how much it made you very afraid of authority figures, how it made you feel like you couldn't trust anyone. If you are now 40, and that abuse caused you to shy away from deeper, meaningful relationships. Well, compared to someone who had a loving childhood and went along to have a great career, a loving spouse, and children, and there you are, you have found yourself alone, not so successful, never having any great relationships, depression, alcohol abuse... Well, that is a lot of happiness that you have missed out on in your life, a lot of missed love and stability. To forgive your parents would mean to process all of that lost happiness, the love you didn't get as a child, and as an adult, your alcohol problems, depression and so forth (and all sorts of lesser consequences obviously). And this example, of course is assuming that that specific abuse was the main trauma in your life, just using it as a simple exercise. So to forgive your parents, mother or father, you would need to first allow all of that pain to surface, with as much detail as possible, not falling in love, not having someone close to you, being afraid of vulnerability and intimacy, everything you have lost because of that, the years of feeling ashamed and bruised. That is a lot, and will most likely require taking forgiveness in steps, not all at the same time. To wake up one day and say I forgive my parents, just like that, without processing the fullness of the pain, you will end up repressing most of it, and even worse, it will be like making yourself believe it is gone and done with. But the result is like locking the pain into a vault and throwing away the key. Then you think you are moving on with your life, but instead you have greatly contributed to your Ego/Ega.

> *"To forgive is to set a prisoner free and discover that the prisoner was you..."* – **Lewis B. Smedes**

Forgiveness is a very powerful tool for freedom and transformation, but it must be done with care, with love, and a lot of understanding. And the more there is to forgive, the more pain will be required to process before the forgiveness can be completed. But without forgiving, you can pretty much forget emotional maturity, unless you have had an awesome life, with little to forgive to anyone, but really, is there anyone who has that little to forgive in our modern societies?

How do you forgive?

Open yourself up to your feelings, talk to the person, in person, or even on your own, practice if you need to. Say something like "you know what you did, well, it hurt me this way or that, it took away my self-worth, my self-confidence, and that made me shy away from bigger career objectives, education, from making friends, from building deeper relationships. And that sucks, really, so much pain from the experience, and I wanted to let you know. I'm not holding it against you, no one is perfect, but it did cause me so much pain, and now I need to let go, I've carried it for long enough, I forgive you".

Put it in your own words, for your own situation, take the time it requires, **allow your heart, your feelings, to guide you**. Stay safe, if facing the person is too triggering for you, then don't, or do it by phone or email. Again, forgiving is not forgetting, it is not wiping the slate clean, to allow them to abuse you again, to start over from scratch. You keep the memory of it, you learn, but you let go of the pain, and again, you do it for you first and foremost. If you feel the relationship can be made better, to be salvaged, or get back with the person, then allow that possibility, but don't sacrifice yourself for it. Make sure the person understands that it is not giving them the chance to do it again, and if the person starts, you will not tolerate it any longer.

Some people might take well to your forgiveness, and actually open up to it, to learn themselves and maybe offer an apology for their behavior, or forgive *you* for something that might have caused *them* pain. It often is like that in relationships, you cause a bit of pain, then they might become a bit careless of causing you pain, then again, a little bit more, until it becomes too big to manage. In those situations, relationships can grow so much, become much more connected once at least one person opens themselves up to honest communications, starting with forgiveness. And also, forgiveness is not all about huge things, you can start small, get the hang of it. All the little things are important too, open yourself up to the wisdom of your heart and let it guide you in regards to what might be stuck, and in need of being let go of.

And, on the other side, making amends, *asking* for forgiveness, which goes hand in hand. Again, **it is not always about what others have done to us, but what we have done to them also**, so to practice forgiveness, is also to practice apologizing for our own stuff, our own actions, and

asking for forgiveness. There is a lot of strength to be gained by doing that, and returning to my "go-to" statement; it is also quite necessary to build up emotional maturity.

"The willingness to forgive is a sign of spiritual and emotional maturity. It is one of the great virtues to which we all should aspire. Imagine a world filled with individuals willing both to apologize and to accept an apology. Is there any problem that could not be solved among people who possessed the humility and largeness of spirit and soul to do either – or both – when needed?..." – **Gordon B. Hinckley**

Keep in mind that some people might object to you telling them they caused you pain, the very notion of that will make them angry, resentful. It might make it harder for you to carry on, but you can still forgive them, or maybe allow it a bit of time and try again later. For some things, you might not be ready to forgive, or to ask for forgiveness, and that's okay too. But avoid saying things like "I will, or can, *never* forgive that person for what they did to me", that just makes you close off a part of your heart not only to them, but to everyone, including you. If the thought of it is too painful, just tell yourself you are not ready to forgive that person. But at least allow the idea of forgiving them within your heart, to intend to come back to it later, maybe even years later if necessary, that's okay. Leaving that intent in your heart can work out the knots surrounding the pain, to break it off into smaller chunks that you can deal with over time. But don't push it aside completely and convince yourself you can never, ever do it, **that will be *your* loss, not theirs**. Some of you might have experienced terrible pain and suffering at the hands of others, and I know it can be hard to forgive, keep in mind it is your own love that hangs in the balance, take the time you need, but don't let it fester in your system for too long. Refusing to forgive only results in refusing to love, and will keep your energies stuck with the people you refuse to forgive, maintaining very unhealthy bonds that will keep you in suffering and torment.

There is great power to be had from fully embodying and processing the pain that a person might have caused you, but to forgive anyway... It requires a great deal of strength and bravery, and you will be the better for it in many ways, what is to gain can never be had with any amount of fortune or fame.

Anger, shame, blame, resentment, all sorts of things can block us from wanting to forgive, or to blind us away from it, so we must be persistent.

And, **you also need to forgive yourself,** for any mistakes, for decisions that you feel were not so great, for imperfections, things you might be ashamed of, allowing yourself to fall into bad relationships... Many people don't think they need to forgive themselves, as it might not make sense to them, but we do, really. **I would say that *you* are the first person that you should practice your forgiveness on**, who else is more deserving of it? Forgiving yourself for decisions you have made, of taking the easy path instead of going through your fears and aiming for something better, being too hard on yourself, or too easy at times, not choosing the right career, focusing on material things instead of love, "stupid" mistakes, getting involved in romantic relationships too early in life, all of that.

When you choose to forgive yourself, you can let go of all sorts of bad energies circling around your internal systems, a path to greater freedom.

> *"All major religious traditions carry basically the same message; that is love, compassion and forgiveness, the important thing is they should be part of our daily lives..."*
> **– Dalai Lama**

Why can it be so hard to forgive at times? Pride, false modesty, shame, arrogance, vanity, greed, jealousy, entitlement, fear...

Remember, the devil is in the details, and those little details become the monsters in our closet, the ones we need to contend with, to face, and to eradicate before we even get to deal with our skeletons. The more of them you have, the less you will be prone to want to open up that closet door, as the terror will be too overwhelming.

So, though forgiveness is a more tangible process, we also need to understand the related elements to it, in association with love and our ever important healing journey out of the illusory Matrix, into life. That is our "rebirth" in a way, as for the Phoenix to be reborn from the ashes of its former life it must suffer the purifying flames first, a painful but necessary process.

On Shame and Blame

Toxicity fills the air, the stench is overwhelming, choking even, crushing despair, killing off your soul little by little, the plants are drying up, mold overgrowth everywhere, peeling paint... Those are the ruinous consequences of inviting shame and blame into your castle, a very cataclysmic duo.

You think I'm kidding? Shame and blame are destroyers of love, some of the main tools of oppression that you have at your disposal, not that you should ever use them, but many do without even knowing it, or without knowing the extent of the pain they can cause.

Okay, so really, the soul *cannot* be killed, it is just a metaphor, you know, a dramatic setup to catch people's attention. And those that don't believe in a soul, that's okay too, but that doesn't leave you off the hook. Regardless of your beliefs, emotional trauma and psychological dysfunctions are real, and their impact are devastating to whatever you think life is, or should be, about.

But, even though the soul cannot be killed, our relationship with our soul can, and does, diminish. So for us, *it is* as if our soul dies, to us anyway, a little at a time the more trauma we have and accumulate, and the more we allow things like shame and blame to distance ourselves from it, from our deeper selves.

Again, I wish I could convey to everyone just how much shame pulls them away from all sort of good things in life, the extent of the damage it does, the better paths it leads them away from. How people often end up settling for way less than they could, simply because of the shame that is hanging over them like a big dark cloud. And a lot of that shame goes unnoticed by most.

"Shame corrodes the very part of us that believes we are capable of change..." – **Brené Brown**

Brené Brown has done a lot of good work on shame and vulnerability, she has written many books on those subjects, done Ted Talks, and has a lot of videos available online, check her out!

What trauma does, again, it is like a piece of you, of your soul, gets locked into a prison of time, in that same situation that you were not able to deal with properly. That is the "trauma" part, a part of you separated from the whole, unwell, wounded. As your soul is perfect, or whatever you want to call that "good" part of you, then anything that is imperfect cannot be contained with the "good", so it gets cast out, away from the present. Those parts of you which you then deny, get afraid of, run away from. With shame (and blame), you basically look at those parts of you as if they are bad, as if they are *not* you at all, and you end up rejecting your "selves" over and over. Those parts of you which you then believe are unworthy of your everyday self, of your "love", casting them so far away into your subconscious, they wither away to near death. That is how we can live such separate lives, from the ideal version of us we try to keep together, and the other parts of us we try to forget, we end up living in limbo, somewhere in between those two versions of us.

Those parts that we reject, that are lost in time, become our "imperfect" children that we try to hide from everyone. As if those parts of you aren't suffering enough, being burdened by the pains of the past, but you then reject them, and doing so, you reject *yourself* little by little, part by part.

That is why shame in possibly the worst in regards to how we see ourselves, our own relationship.

Rejecting ourselves has of course very deep consequences to our sense of self, and if people think that they don't reject themselves when they feel shame, they do, again, as we are not simply a "whole" being, we are made in parts, our energies are not simply "one" thing. We are made up of all of our experiences, all our conditioning, our thoughts, our morals, our trauma, our dreams... The more shame you feel about this or that experience or behavior, the more of *you* you end up rejecting, **too embarrassed about those parts for even *you* to love and feel compassion for**, that is very sad, and very life depriving. The best life is lived in full love and mastery of our internal parts, only then can we *be* love, and only then will the universe start to open up to your dreams, to have the law of attraction work for you. Shame is maybe the worst feeling to have for yourself when considering the higher things that life can offer to anyone. It is like the "anti" law of attraction, shame, followed by blame and regret.

Fear and hatred get mixed up in those emotions, then life becomes very dull, no meaning, no purpose, always just "getting by". Maybe financial and career success can still be possible, but not love, not a deeper sense of purpose, those will always go unfulfilled. In fact, all trauma works against the law of attraction, as all trauma works against love and a relationship with your true self.

Again, the idea that we are not whole, that we are made up of fractured parts, consider that when you blame yourself, **who is blaming whom**? Which part of you is blaming which other part of you? One part who thinks he/she is perfect (or better), blaming another part of you that the perfect part thinks is a screw up? Same as shame, parts of you thinking that the stuff that other parts of you have done or experienced is shameful, and then those parts become rejected. But in a way, all those parts are you, tearing each other "apart", creating more fractured selves in the process. Then "you" become less present, less whole, and less capable of love. Your inner battlefield becomes very messy, with so many casualties, and all of them are you, parts of you. And again, trying to go into one better direction in life becomes much more difficult, as so many parts of you are not "on board", they not only *not* contribute to the journey, but end up working against it despite themselves.

AS AN EXERCISE: Try to consider it that way, when you feel blame or shame, who is blaming who, which part of you is shaming which other part of you? It might give you some insights as to what is going on inside, the internal wars and conflicts that wear you down, and what you need to do to figure things out, to heal, and to get those parts talking and communicating with one another in a healthy way, to mend their relationship. Open up a dialogue with yourself, or with your "selves", like "Part of me is blaming, or shaming, another part of me, what is going on? I would like to understand, and stop doing that. I'm feeling it has something to do with (so and so), maybe because of when...", in your own words, for your situation. And try to feel who is blaming whom, and why, and who is getting blamed, and why, to feel from their point of view. It can be a very enlightening experience.

Regret and Guilt

If there is one thing that will pull you right out of the present moment time and time again, it's regret, that's the whole idea of it, to reflect in a negative manner things of the past, that we have done, or not done, experienced or not experienced. Regret is an energy just as with anything else in this universe, frequencies and vibrations, and this particular energy cancels out your ability to be in the now at a great degree, it acts kind of like an "anti-focus/anti-present" force field. Many of the other negative emotions also have that effect, well, all of them really, but I would say regret is the worst of them. For every little thing you regret, part of you checks out of the present, away from life, away from the relationship you are trying to build with yourself, and surrenders to the darkened abyss of your subconscious. Love, gratitude and compassion work in the opposite manner, their energies increase your ability to be in the present, to be fully embodied in your being.

"Of all the words of mice and men, the saddest are, "It might have been"..." – **Kurt Vonnegut**

Guilt often makes us regret, so they go well together, not in a "good" well kind of way, more like two miserable little friends spending their lives drowning their sorrows in the neighborhood pub as life passes them by day by day. They so much long for the release of death, that they willfully allow death to hang over them, to pull them into it while their bodies are still alive.

Trauma is not fun, and we should not blame anyone for not having the courage to face it, and as many people are not even aware of the pain they carry, how can we blame? We are all in the same boat, the more we understand, the more we share our strength with other people, the more we can become aware and have better tools to face those things that go bump in our subconscious.

"Guilt is the total of All the negative feelings we have had about ourselves, any form of self-hatred, self-rejection, feelings of worthlessness, sinfulness, inferiority, incompetence, failure or emptiness. The feeling that there are things in us that are lacking or missing or incomplete..."
– Ken Wapnick

Now, some people think that regret and guilt are great (and even shame), as they are "harsh lessons of life, reminders" that serve to prevent people from "doing it again", such are the tools of emotionally immature parents and ineffective leaders. I will say that *at times*, temporary guilt and regret can help us to process things that we have done, can help us to "feel" the proper emotions that we might not have experienced in the first place, or with hindsight, to re-evaluate things of the past. And also they can help to keep our Ego in check, to not allow it to inflate like the big hot air balloon it can be, to lift us off the ground of reality and have us live in the fog. But the guilt and regret should only be temporary, and for the purpose of healing, overcoming, and possibly seeing/feeling from the eyes and heart of other people, how they might have been affected by our words or actions, or us from theirs. So while reflecting on all those feelings, shame, regret, guilt and such, it can point us in the direction of what we need to heal, and how to go about it, but for the purpose of moving on, not staying in those feeling. So again, it should only be a temporary means to a great end.

The healing journey has a lot to do with letting go of regrets, guilt, shame and blame, to forgive ourselves for all our transgressions, and to forgive others for theirs. Facing those things can represent at times a very steep climb to becoming emotionally mature, but we must, otherwise many parts of us will remain lingering in the past forever.

Vulnerability and Gratitude

Without vulnerability, relationships, and life, are like fading flowers, wilted lettuce, all of our surroundings become dull and decaying. Then we see no other alternative than to focus on material gain and success, as everything else that we would desire seems unattainable, or hidden from our sight.

When you don't allow yourself to be vulnerable, you block things from other people. And at some level, we all know when that happens, we can see the lack of transparency in other people's eyes, or feel it in our hearts. We often dismiss it, we make ourselves believe it isn't there, and it can also provide us with an excuse to do the same, an excuse to not face the stuff we would rather not face. And when we do see it in others, it makes us think we can't be vulnerable ourselves. If *they* hide stuff, maybe we can't trust them, then *we* hide stuff, then they also feel it and believe they can't trust *us*, and the darkness keeps getting darker. Relationships will always be very limited as long as people don't allow themselves to open up, or do things to make the other person feel that they shouldn't.

Yes, our fear of emotional pain is strong, it often blocks us in many ways, especially from allowing healthy vulnerability, but to overcome those fears can be one of the greatest gifts of life.

What does vulnerability look like?

First, it is not weakness, it is not frailty, it is not allowing yourself to be taken advantage of, it is not putting yourself up to be ridiculed or belittled, and it is not about having a "bleeding heart". True vulnerability is about allowing yourself to be you, not the ego part of you, anyone can do that, but **the authentic you**, the *you* you might be ashamed of at times, the *you* that has strong opinions that are sometimes controversial, the *you* that is afraid of the dark, the *you* that has the courage to express your feelings even if people might disparage or denigrate them. Having strong and healthy boundaries is a must if a person wants to open themselves to being truly vulnerable, as some people will try to take advantage of what you share of yourself. But to know that you can deal with it, to know when people are trying to mess with you, and say no thanks, that will increase your ability, your resolve, to know true vulnerability, which is the only way you can know true love.

An openness to explore, and to be explored, without the fears that most people are fettered by.

Healthy vulnerability in a relationship can be the greatest experience, and a lack of vulnerability can feel so dreadful, like death itself. To be with someone that allows a great deal of vulnerability means that they know who they are, and are not afraid of showing themselves *as is*, the good, the bad, even those parts they might not even know yet of themselves. It can be a true gift for two people who allow themselves to be deeply vulnerable with one another, and a means to explore the things that you might not even know are there.

"Love comes when manipulation stops; when you think more about the other person than about his or her reactions to you. When you dare to reveal yourself fully. When you dare to be vulnerable..." – **Dr. Joyce Brothers**

Some people believe that "grown ups" must be guarded and "strong" for all sorts of reasons. Many relinquish their ability to remain open and vulnerable, and along with those losses, so does authenticity and empathy follow the same path. As if openness is only for the innocence of childhood, yet how can love find anyone who barricades themselves behind thick walls and impenetrable force fields?

Writing this book is an exercise in vulnerability, to share my opinions, my knowledge, to have people judge, connect to, or reject what I share, my own journey, not such an easy thing, I needed to build up to it, and to let go.

Real vulnerability and authenticity builds character (the good kind of character, not the ego kind), and increases our E.M. by opening ourselves up to the world, and accepting the potential fall outs. On the road to getting there, there will be a period of trial and error as we test out how people react to the vulnerability we allow ourselves. The ones with low E.M., that could not be vulnerable for the life of them, will most likely tease, sarcasm, act out against your vulnerability, as it will feel like a threat to them. It will either remind them of just how much they can't allow themselves to be vulnerable, or they might think you will ask them to be vulnerable in return, or they might just want to take advantage of you. But it is one way to sort out who you can trust, and who you can't. There might be pain along the way, but the opportunities for growth are great. Those that consistently take advantage of your vulnerability, abuse you, hurt you, have no business remaining in your social circle.

Take the cue, and do what you must. The solution is *not* to stop being vulnerable, it is to remove those that will not support you in your vulnerability out of your life. There is no deep connection to be made with people that don't allow vulnerability, or work against it, plain and simple.

And that goes for love, compassion, empathy, trust... All go together, pillars that stand tall against any storm. Remove any one of them, and the others will soon falter.

I understand it can be hard to be honest and vulnerable at times, fully honest, for a host of reasons, sometimes from selfishness, sometimes by trying to be caring for another, at times we would prefer to be honest, but we lack the courage or the vulnerability, then fears set in... Again, be kind to yourself, the idea is to improve, not to be perfect. Understanding the reasons why we choose not to be honest, towards others or others towards us, and have compassion for those "dishonest" interactions, and tolerate parts of it for the right reasons. That is one more element to the journey we must accept and contend with.

Gratitude

To have full, authentic gratitude is to express love for who you are and where you are in life, *all* of it. To not differentiate into "good" or "bad" categories, to not judge, but to accept your life *as is*, to see and feel the experiences as they come into your life, to learn from, and grow from... Not such an easy thing, right? So, like with everything else, don't expect perfection, enjoy the gains, and don't get hung up too much for the losses.

Forgiveness can open doors to love, it can remove the obstructions to it, but to *sustain* love within us, we must be able to feel gratitude on a regular basis. To appreciate life is to love, and to love is to appreciate life. And how can appreciation even exist without gratitude? If a person is not capable of appreciation and gratitude, then healing from their past trauma becomes very difficult, if not impossible. If a person has nothing in their lives to feel grateful for, then hope is lost, and love becomes a forlorn notion.

Increasing vulnerability and gratitude, and decreasing shame and guilt, are maybe the most powerful ways of increasing our capacity for true, unconditional love, the path to loving ourselves fully. We cannot force compassion into our being, nor love, those come gradually and naturally once we remove the barriers to them. And every bit of gratitude we can summon up can be like heat seeking missiles to those barriers, destroying them where they stand, and freeing the parts stuck behind them.

"Gratitude is the healthiest of all human emotions. The more you express gratitude for what you have, the more likely you will have even more to express gratitude for..." – **Zig Ziglar**

Gratitude is seeing and feeling things for their beauty and how enriching to your life they are, a means to invite love into your being and direct it towards something specific that you can understand and focus on. It helps to demystify the process of tuning your system to healthier energies. When you have earned the ability to be moved to tears without shame when seeing beauty in this world, be it a sunset, children playing, a truly caring gesture, or even a challenge or suffering that you have overcome or seen the positive contribution to your life, **then you know you are on your way to true love and emotional maturity**, and inching towards an even a higher state, *Emotional Wisdom*.

EXERCISES TO DEVELOP GRATITUDE: Here are a few exercises to practice gratitude. They can be as easy as expressing thanks for waking up in the morning, yes, even if just for being alive, or about some bad experience you have had and your ability to let go, forgiving someone, or someone forgiving you, a promotion, a person being kind to you out of the blue... This list of things to be grateful for can be endless when we start opening ourselves up to seeing things as they are, and the positive contributions to our lives they can have.

It is a way of building up positive connections in your system to offset the often negative thinking processes of the mind, and the effects of trauma and emotional dysfunctions. So to "reformat" your being to be better able to tune into higher forms of energy, kind of like re-engineering a radio so that it can pick up channels you would prefer to have, rather than just the local news and endless advertisements that contribute to keeping you in low E.M. mode.

This is just a short list to give you a start, I suggest taking the time to make one of your own that makes sense to your particular situation, as you know yourself best, or at least you should. And putting the effort into your own list is a good relationship building exercise from you, to you.

A few minutes of daily practice is all it takes to make a good start of it:

- I am grateful to have an open mind and heart capable of grasping the benefits that love and gratitude can have in my life
- Despite the challenges, I am grateful to be alive and to have opportunities to make my life better
- I am grateful to have understood the impact of some of my childhood abuse/trauma, and have grown the courage to make amends with it
- I am grateful that I can see my interactions with people for how they truly are, how they affect me, and the steps I can take to improve
- I am grateful for the things I have in my life; a roof over my head, food, means to satisfy my basic requirements, friends, family, enough money to pay my bills...

These exercises might seem simplistic, but they work, and the more you practice them, the more you develop gratitude. Just like muscles, if you lift one pound 5 times a day, there will be progress, but you won't see it right away. At some point, gradually, you will move up to 2 pounds, 3 pounds, then more often, and the effect will be seen, and felt, and you *will* become stronger, the results *must* follow the efforts.

The more you practice, the deeper your ability to express gratitude for all things.

FOOD FOR THOUGHT: Also, we can express gratitude for things that might not have quite yet become a reality in our lives, in a way to attract them. Like to express gratitude for our ability to see and feel more clearly, even if there is still more progress to be made on those fronts. Gratitude invites love into our being, and love can pave roads not yet taken by us, to make the journey smoother when we start walking on them. If that reality becomes part of your life, your roads being constructed even before you tread on them, you'll begin to understand what kind of gift a deep expression of gratitude can truly be.

Your own Personal Love Language: Doing "*You*"

How about doing "you" for a while?

Wouldn't that feel just great for a change, no pretense, no wondering what others will think, no masks, fears, just the full unadulterated manifestation of you. Try it out, see how it feels to just be *you*, to say what you feel like, to allow your true expression, and not worry so much about how others might judge. The people that are closest to you should support you in your efforts, if they don't, well, that says a lot. We often repress so much of ourselves, again, to fit in, to not cause potential pain... All sorts of reasons that we need to let go of, as *not* doing you, well, that cost is intrinsically associated to the love you can have for yourself.

"If you aren't good at loving yourself, you will have a difficult time loving anyone, since you'll resent the time and energy you give another person that you aren't even giving to yourself..." – **Barbara De Angelis**

Feelings, nothing more than feelings...

Let me walk you through this: **Everything that we do in life has to do with feelings,** that is what we get out of all of our experiences. Life is not about the details, not about specific goals, money, power, fame, but about how we *feel* in the situations we experience.

If a person books a trip to the south, and they convince themselves it will be miserable if it rains, and if it does, then for them the whole trip was a waste of time and money, all ruined. If it is sunny, it might be the best trip of their lives, all because of their *state of mind*, and how they "felt" about the details once they got there. So our mind is very powerful in regards to perception, and of the quality of life we can have. The more you grow in E.M., the better the connection to your feelings, and the more in control of your emotions, which all contributes to a much better quality of life in so many ways. A person with high E.M. will not convince themselves beforehand that the trip will be a complete waste if it rains, they know they will be able to find something enjoyable to do if it does. And so goes many other details of life, so many things become better, if not everything, with higher emotional maturity, without even anything changing, same details, different perception of them. And the improvements you make in life, of your "details", only makes things even better than what they already feel to you.

So, to manage to heal, to become more whole, for all of your parts to consciously and conscientiously work towards a unifying goal, all of your systems, all of your efforts, feelings and emotions, actions and thoughts, all focusing in a sustained trajectory, a path that is just the right fit for who you are, and what you are capable of... Then what matters of details, rain of shine, it will all "feel" right to you.

If that is not a dream come true, well, not sure what is...

"You are all things. Denying, rejecting, judging or hiding from any aspect of your total being creates pain and results in a lack of wholeness..." – **Joy Page**

To Become Whole

To become whole within yourself, for your mind and thoughts to understand what your emotions and feelings are going through, a whole body communication system, all on the same page communicating the same information that all components within yourself can understand and process, that is wholeness, a fully realized being. Those are the fruits of the labors described within these pages. The work is not complete of course, but the idea of it remains...

That language, that all encompassing communication vocabulary, not only within you, but how your being interacts with the world around you, is a greater part of this journey. To get all of "you" working together, removing any impurities, all things that impede your systems from working together in harmony. Then your whole being becomes your "I", your awareness, and not just a vague presence in your brain, or in your mind.

To not follow this path, it can be like a doctor trying to assess the pains of a child who does not have much of a vocabulary to explain anything. The doctor puts a finger somewhere, and asks the child if it hurts, then tries other places. When the doctor finds a sore spot, the doctor asks if it feels hot, if it feels cold, or like nails... It can be extremely difficult to treat a child who cannot properly communicate. But the efforts, trying to develop a means of communication between them, we *must* do the same with all of our internal parts. Just like for letting go of the pain, the more we can "put a finger" on it, to give it a proper name, the more we can heal it out of our being. Our system is intelligent, but it requires our help, **our permission of sorts to do the work**. If a parent asks a 3 year old what they want for supper, and the child responds with "that" without pointing to anything, simply because one time she pointed to something in the fridge and her mother said "that?", and the child responded yes. Then for her, that thing is simply "that". But without being in front of the fridge, and the mother not making anything of the reference, she can't give her child what she wants. Your system is the same, if you can't understand what you don't want, and what you do want, it can't help you with anything. That is part of the reason why our pain gets stuck, and remains stuck. The vocabulary between the dissociated memory and emotions is lacking, or we have forgotten it, repressed it, or are afraid to face it. Either way, the gap remains.

To develop a communal language of reference for yourself, you can start with trying to understand your emotions better by having a dialogue with your "selves", as if those emotions come from different parts of you, and you are trying to understand, to say things to yourself such as "I hear you", "I can feel you", "I'm not sure what you are trying to make me aware of, but I feel some anger, I don't really know why, but I want to know", "I have ignored you long enough, and I want to stop doing that"... You can be amazed as to what the intelligence of your being is capable of when you open yourself up to a true relationship with yourself, to understand that you are not a "whole" person, you are not just "one" indivisible being, so to treat those "divisions" as unique parts with their own concerns, fears, and struggles, your emotional growth can skyrocket.

You can do this especially when you get triggered into emotions and feelings that are difficult to manage, like with a partner, a family member or a friend. Don't be shy to explain to the other person what you are doing, they might learn a thing or two. And have compassion with all of who you are, all those parts, even the ones you don't like so much, you will need to learn how to love them to become emotionally mature. You are the one all those internal parts are looking up to, hoping to come alive for and with, to free themselves of the pains of the past, the dysfunctional programming, the dreams not yet fulfilled, to live in the present as one big happy internal family. Then when you put your mind and heart to task towards a certain goal, you become that unstoppable force moving through the ocean of doubt and fears most people are stuck in, the head above the crowd, the light that shines as bright as the sun.

"Your self-talk is the channel of behavior change..."
– Gino Norris

But if you never practice that emotional language, learning how to express what you are actually feeling, if most of the time you respond to situations with "I'm fine", "that's okay", or continuously repress, or misinterpret, your emotions for whatever reason, if you do that 80-90% of the time like many people do, either in the belief they are being polite, or to not "rock the boat", draw attention to themselves. Then how can you ever think you will be able to understand yourself, to know what you are truly feeling if most of the time you repress that process. **You can't behave one way 90% of the time, then expect that delicate system of expression within you to comply anytime you demand to know certain feelings**, or even to have the capacity for love and compassion, we don't work that way. It is a work in progress, and to build your personal relationship requires care and dedication, otherwise, well, sad to say, you'll need to learn how to accept a mundane kind of existence. Maybe you'll get rich and have lots of money to distract yourself from that reality, parties, bling, cars and so forth, but deep down, you will know the truth of it anytime you stop long enough to feel the little pangs of lost hope deep inside. Yes, those little details add up, there is a cost to not saying how you truly feel, no matter how good the reasons you think you have.

MUSICAL INTERLUDE: Try this one, **Difference Maker**, by *Need to Breathe,* kind of sums up a lot of stuff, and the *whys* of it all.

A true gift in life is to be able to express yourself in all of your colors, shapes and sizes with others who do the same, not only of them allowing you that expression, but encouraging it with their own caring expressive behaviors.

Do you believe there's a greater reason to life than your own true expression and what gets created out of it?

Feeling understood can be an underrated pleasure, and most people don't truly understand how much they crave to feel just that, understood, but not in terms of politics, sports teams, career objectives, but deeply understood, feelings, emotions, heart-based attunement between people. That might be the biggest "bonus" of living in a small supportive community, you don't need to explain yourself, you are accepted as you are, you are known for most of yourself. And you don't need to make excuses for any of your strengths or weaknesses, no need to hide, nor any need to project false images. Wouldn't that be grand to live like that, with everyone you meet on a daily basis? You know who they are, they know who you are, no need to worry about anything... And feeling understood to your own self, all of your parts making sense to you, all of your desires, aspirations, your past, your present and future, all communicating in the same language. To get a taste of that, is to never go back to the wild wild west of our dysfunctional Ego/Ega where the rules of love and life do not apply.

The Importance of Journaling

Journaling takes things one step further, the effort of writing out your feelings, what they are associated to, to put it down on paper, or in your computer, adds an extra dimension to sort things out.

Consider self-talk, journaling and other similar exercises to develop your own personal emotional vocabulary as an attempt of the "you" that is in the present moment to communicate with the other parts of you that are not. The ones that have different opinions, that are stuck in fantasies, in prisons in time, in past events, in trauma...

Again, thinking about yourself as different parts of a whole, one part wanting to take off and live on a sailboat for a few years, another part wanting to focus on a career, another part can't wait for retirement, another part just wants to play music, another part wants to be in a long term relationship, another part wants to be single, and the list goes on. We often think of all of those parts as *us*, and most people don't give this a second thought. But think about it, one part wants to be in a long term relationship, and another part wants to keep being single, for the freedom it provides. Those are two very conflicted feelings competing against one another, how can anyone think of themselves as "one" when there are parts so opposed within them? If every person was just "one" being, no conflict could ever exist inside of them. And all of the conflicts I mentioned, was just present day stuff, consider all your parts that are stuck in the past, replaying trauma, still not over the bullying, still not over the abuse, not over the regrets... Those again are all parts that conflict with the whole, they have their own separate reality, their own separate needs and desires, which all prevents us from truly moving in one firm direction in life.

Journaling is about understanding yourself better, to understand what those other parts want, to understand your fears, your blockages, and to get all your parts on board understanding one another. It can help to sort through conflicting ideas, like one part would like to live on an island, and another part wants to live in the city, to "talk it out", and choose one over the other, a final say in the matter to stop draining energies that are flowing in opposed directions, wasting efforts trying to create things that will never be as long as the conflicts persist.

Journaling your day: Think about emotional situations, situations when you wanted to say something, but you held back, when your co-worker took credit for something you did, when your boss asked you to work during the weekend, when that cute girl, or guy, gave you a smile on the bus, when you tripped on the sidewalk and felt embarrassed for thinking of yourself as clumsy... Those are all great things to journal about, not only to reconcile your various feelings, to make sure they don't accumulate into repressed feelings, but also to understand the feelings that are already repressed, the wounds and trauma of your past, and all the nuances of what those emotions were when you felt them. Maybe journaling about how you felt when your co-worker took credit for your work will remind you of a similar experience in school when your friend did the same thing, and it was very traumatic to you, as not only did you work so hard for it, but your friend broke your trust, and from then on you have had a hard time making/trusting friends. Maybe journaling about how embarrassed you were of tripping on the sidewalk will remind you of all the times your mother of father called you clumsy for similar situations. Those feelings that you can pull up when journaling, especially when deeply repressed, can help you to finally get over them, to process them in a healthy way, and finally rid yourself of embarrassment, issues with trust, and all sorts of other blockages you might have.

"The starting point of discovering who you are, your gifts, your talents, your dreams, is being comfortable with yourself. Spend time alone. Write in a journal..."
– Robin Sharma

Here is a fictional example of a journal entry, to give you an idea: "On my way to work this morning I tripped again on that corner of the sidewalk that is broken, the city people should really fix it before someone breaks their ankle, or falls into traffic, maybe I'll call them again tomorrow. That guy that seems interested in me, that I cross paths with every now and then was there, he saw me tripping, must think I'm a total klutz. Can't imagine him ever randomly asking me out after that public display of just how not a lady I am. I'm thinking now, so many times when I was growing up, my father kept calling me a klutz every time I tripped, or dropped something, made me feel so bad, and seems like he purposefully did it even more when there were other people around, why would a father do that to his own little girl, it was as if he took joy in calling me that, like he wanted me to drop something, or fall to the ground, aching for an opportunity to make him feel better about himself, more superior. I can't believe I forgot all of that, and here I am, calling *myself* a klutz anytime I am less than perfect, and making myself feel like I am not a "proper" woman because of that. Like I haven't had enough of my father constantly calling me that word? I should make an effort to never call myself that again, I hate that word, shame on him for drilling it into me, he's the one that should be called a klutz for actually taking pleasure in my suffering, an emotional klutz."

Journaling can be a very powerful tool to not only heal from the past and to make sense of your today, but also to help you build a greater relationship with yourself, the now version, and the future version you would like to become. Kind of like active self-therapy, and the more you do it, the better you get, and the deeper you can go. And don't worry about how good you can write, or how much sense it makes, just do it for yourself, and accept what comes of it. When we allow ourselves to revisit the past, our relationships, our parenting, only in our minds, it can help, but when we do it on paper, it has an additional power to "exorcise our demons", it makes it more real.

In the beginning, it might be a bit difficult to see those words on paper, or on your computer, but keep in mind you are doing it for yourself, and if you need to delete, or burn, what you have written, then do that. Sometimes it is hard to externalize our deepest thoughts, even when we are alone in our own house, or room, seeing it appear in "reality" can be scary, but that is where the power comes from, to overcome our fears and say "that's what happened to me" or "that's how I truly feel", it becomes real. And as the reality sinks in, you are better able to process the emotions that are attached to those things.

So start journaling, and either keep it nice and safe hidden somewhere, locked in your computer, or get rid of it when you are done, whichever you feel more comfortable with, as long as you dare to say everything that your heart needs to express.

Drawing: Drawing can be even a more powerful tool to communicate with your subconscious, it can be daunting when your drawings are not so great, but at least give it a try and see if it works for you.

The Value of Intent in Everything that you do

Intent... I have mentioned it before, but I wish to do so again here. Intent is to the heart what will is to the mind, together they dictate what you *do* in life. And if there is one thing that is so often dismissed and misunderstood, again, it is that, intent.

What drives us forward other than intent?

Think about it, intent decides pretty much *everything* that we do in life, what we build, what we get out of bed for, the relationships we create and maintain. If we have no intent, not even to pay our bills or put food in the refrigerator, then we have no purpose, we just lay on our sofas and fall into depression. You get up with the intent to relieve your bladder, you eat with an intent to satisfy your appetite, there is intent behind every word we speak, behind every action, and even behind every thought.

Yet, what do people really know about the intents that drive every action they undertake?

People that are very driven, that have taken the time to know who they are, what they want, that understand their feelings and emotions, that have managed to heal a great part of their trauma and wounds (or didn't have so much to begin with), can have incredible resolve in moving forwards in life, to whatever goal they have set for themselves. Their intent is clear, their will is strong, **they know what they want, and why they want it**. Most people never achieve that state, as they know too little of themselves, and they know too little of the intent that drives them day by day. The more we can direct our intent to one greater goal, the more all of our efforts and energies will guide us along that path, to pull us to that destination.

"Intentional living is the art of making our own choices before others' choices make us..." – **Richie Norton**

Without clear intent, we drift, and strong will cannot become part of our lives. With low E.Q./E.M., our intents are oftens hidden from us, they get diverted into the past, the future, selfish purposes and desires, food and comfort, routines. That is why people with very low E.Q./E.M. can hardly ever rise up in their jobs (unless by who they know), but on their own means, they just can't. They are often at the bottom rungs of society, they suffer from addictions, they either end up being very abusive, or being abused. The more we rise in E.M., the more we understand ourselves, the more we can understand our intents, which can lead us to our purpose. And not only to know our purpose, but to have the strength and courage to make the sacrifices, to do the work, to make it happen.

Though it is important that you understand the basics of intent, and how it is related to will and purpose, you don't really need to worry about it directly, it will come to you the more you free yourself from your emotional dysfunctions and develop a better relationship with your full being, it is part of the process. Though the workings of intent are the same for everyone, not everyone derives their intent from the same ideas and notions. Our beliefs, our desires, and our environment all have an impact on our intent, what we value, and what we aim for in life. And with greater E.M., our intent naturally develops towards helping others.

What Defines you

In relationship to will and intent, you should also consider what you allow to define you on your path; such as clothes, house, car, career, friends, culture, beliefs, habits, preferences, tastes... Those things that you allow to define you can end up confining you, strings holding you down. Like Gulliver, those little people could not hold him by themselves, but, while he was unconscious, they managed to keep him captive with their little strings. If you get enough sewing thread, however thin it might be, you could hold down even an elephant if you're willing to put the work into it.

Those strings for us, they are energetic connections, and they do in fact hold us in place in so many ways, they hold us to people (bonding/attuning), to our past, to our possessions, to our memories, to our emotions... **They guide our lives in unseen, but very real ways**. Every single wound/trauma, anyone you have not forgiven, all your aspirations and desires that might be pulling you in many different directions (again, be careful what you wish for), all attachments to your belongings and your routines, things you say that you "can't live without", imagine the devastating messages you send to your subconscious when you say that... Just that one thing, "I can't live without this or that", can confine your life in many dreadful ways. What if you say that you can't live without coffee, so any kind of life that would lead you away from a source of coffee becomes out of the question, or any threat to coffee production feels like a little death to you, or a big one depending on how much you have conditioned your subconscious to believe you really can't live without it... Multiply this by the hundreds, notions, fears, beliefs... Then you can see why your life, to make any change, any progress, can be so complicated and heart wrenching when you don't understand what you are fighting against.

That is life, the "Devil" is in the details, so skip the details... With your heart that is, don't invest your heart in the details, in things, the past, the "bad" stuff, just invest your heart in the goals you desire, and let the rest work itself out. Otherwise you will be like Gulliver, not physically, but your emotional being, your heart, will be kept tied down and freedom will be forever out of reach.

"Every job is composed of many small details, any one of which, if overlooked, can create big problems later..."
– Napoleon Hill

Those little things that bog down the healthy functioning of our heart, of our capacity to love, think about all the ways that they shape our world: What motives do lawmakers have when they create new laws, selfish, self-serving, temporary means to achieve some kind of goal, or are they capable of more compassion, to think about the future direction and well being of their country, of the world? What about politicians, the decisions they make on a daily basis, more loving, or more fearful, thinking about their election, or of making the right choices? Police, education systems, all levels of governments, from the ones at the bottom of the ladder, stealing office supplies and forcing the company to take tougher measures and treat everyone as a possible thief, or people willing to help others, all the way to the top floors. Everyone making decisions, for themselves, and others, more loving, or more selfish, more compassion, or more jealousy... Doctors prescribing mounds of drugs for the kickbacks they get, or ones that refuse to play the game. People accepting to work for tobacco companies, or those who refuse to do so.

Lawyers taking on frivolous lawsuits, and even the military: Do you want someone in charge of our forces who looks at billions worth of weapons that are nearing their shelf life (or fancy new ones to try out), and begins to wonder about where to start a little war to not have them "go to waste", or one that will be happy that the weapons were never used in the first place, and also happy to recycle them?

Yes, those little details are important, very important, and every little bit of extra capacity that people have to love, to develop emotional maturity, has compounded effects. What people have in their hearts, people's agendas, their *intent*, determines what goes on in our world, all contributes to shaping the future of tomorrow. To live in a world were we don't feel we need to compete for every morsel, where you don't have to keep checking your phone or wallet in your back pocket, for women to be able to walk in the streets at night without fears, where children are consistently treated with compassion and respect, well, I believe we can have that, but we, as in *all* of us, need to work for it.

Ventilating and Healthy Angering

As *my* intent was not to go deep into psychology as it goes beyond the grasp of my expertise, and there are numerous professionals and resources to help guide you along that part of the journey regardless. But I still wanted to mention a few words on ventilating and healthy angering, as they can be important tools for you to be aware of, and to use, especially with journaling and self-talk, and potentially with therapists and other supportive people. To allow ourselves to "ventilate", which means to express what we need to express, and in the way we need to express it, alongside healthy angering, can go a very long way to healing our past and properly developing an emotional vocabulary, and also to connect to the realities of your present self, or I should say "selves".

We cannot process emotions properly unless we have a healthy range of emotional capacity within ourselves, and this includes healthy angering and vulnerability. By "healthy angering" I mean to say to use it for the purposes of healing, in a controlled manner, of allowing it on purpose to get the "bad" stuff out, but not to have it control you, nor hurt anyone in the process.

Healthy angering *is not* to blurt out mean things randomly, or use it as an excuse when we can't help ourselves but to throw our frustrations at others.

So for those who already tend to get angry in non-constructive ways, best not to indulge so much in healthy angering, to not give yourself that permission as it can then easily be used as an excuse, at least until you get it under control. Anger can be a double edged sword, so proceed with caution. It can help those that have repressed that form of coping mechanism, which can lead to so much repressed trauma as we need to anger for all sorts of injustices and unfairness we have experienced, but only as a temporary measure. As children (and sometimes in relationships), we are often not allowed to ventilate our frustrations through anger, and that important tool gets repressed. So it is mainly for those people that I suggest reconnecting to your anger, and make proper use of it, especially when you are alone. Not to use it to take your frustrations out on people, like many do.

"Anger expressed in a healthy and positive way means that we channel emotional anger towards resolution not attack..."
– Byron R. Pulsifer

Give yourself the permission to call out anything, from your past, your present, to help find the proper name to your feelings in practice, and also direct them to the proper source. Again, on your own, you can go all out in the way that makes sense to you. And if you are concerned about people you might live with, or neighbors, go out in nature, or bury your face deep in a pillow or two, then let 'her rip!

As children, it is often drilled into us so deep, to not anger, to not swear, to not talk back, especially at our parents, that even when adult, even in the privacy of our own home and alone, we can still not dare to voice out certain words, certain feelings. Your feelings are important, free them from their prisons, develop that relationship with your repressed emotions.

Say it out loud, you suck, you monster, how could you do that to your own daughter, to your own son? You animal, you "insert your own #$#", couldn't you contain your anger, your violence, do you have any idea how shameful of myself it made me? How much I felt unloved, how much it made me not trust anyone, how I could never manage to have a proper relationship for what you did to me? How could you cheat on me, what didn't I give you, why didn't you talk to me about it? Why did you bully me, do you have any idea how scared of school that made me, how my grades slipped, how I ended up dropping out of school, and how I got stuck working at one dead end job after another...

Remember, you are doing this for you, for your love, it is your time, your life. If you can't come up with the proper words and feelings, say that, I wish I had the right words, I wish I could pull out these feelings for what they are. There is power in telling someone "FU, I ain't taking it no more", even if on your own, alone, and voicing it out to an imaginary version of the person, or using a surrogate, either a willing friend, or some object. And yes, *voice it out*, the words, the feelings, need to come out. Also, you can use this process for the small stuff as well, the things you face everyday that can hurt you, or even just irk you, it doesn't have to be all about the biggest wounds.

Don't go out and hurt anyone though, that is not cool, but alone, do whatever, break a dish if you want, just don't hurt yourself either in the process. Physical expression is also a means of developing a certain vocabulary and can help to ventilate, grieve, and move on. Healthy angering can be most useful to express the pains of the past, it can be the single most important factor, that and allowing any feelings, and any words, to express those feelings. Let it out, let it all out...

And allow yourself to cry throughout this process, again, very important...

"I believe there is great beauty in a person breaking down, and allowing themselves to cry the tears they have never allowed themselves to cry before..." – **Me**

A FEW WORDS ON SELF CARE: One of the first things I got into in this book was about being kind to yourself, so as we are heading into the last section, I thought I would get back into it a tad more. I have found it quite useful in my own journey to practice self-care, and not just to "think" about it, but to actually do healthy and loving gestures for myself, and to plan them ahead of time just as we would make plans for a romantic supper or time spent with friends or family. An evening for taking a soothing bath with candles and music, a night out to your favorite place, a walk in the park, take yourself out for an ice cream cone, have a paid or self massage, even if only to nestle under a blanket with a good book on a cold and snowy winter day in your favorite jammies.

And guys, this concerns you as well!

Men are not often into the "self-care" thing that much, but they should, just as much as women. It is about the relationship you build with yourself, all of it, mind, body, emotions. The sensual aspect of our skin, our senses, our whole body, to feel it properly and not just keep using it just as if a mere tool, like a hammer, to get things done.

Also, to heal from the past, to experience myself in a more "clear" way, I have had much success with using cleaning as a mindful exercise, like, actual cleaning of the house or the car, anything. To do it not just as a chore to get over, nor with resentment and negative thoughts, but as if cleaning and decluttering my external environment was connected to cleaning and decluttering my internal environment. It is known that people with messy houses and living environments (and debts, spotty personal hygiene, and messy relationships for that matter) are often just as untidy inside, those go together. As taking care of the messes on the outside, even mere accumulated dust, it forces us to face the clutter inside, *if* we do it in good spirit and intent.

Same as fixing things, sometimes I specifically have a few things on my list of things to fix for the joys it can give me to work on something manually, even just to do something as simple as re-hanging a frame, to take my mind off of things at times when I need to do that, and also how great it makes me feel when it is done, an accomplishment that is real and very visible, opposed to so many things we often do at work that are not clear as to what comes of our efforts, which can contribute to voids in our sense of accomplishment.

Other very good means of self-care and mindful practices: Meditation, regular exercise, anything to raise your heart-rate a few times a week in a healthy manner, yoga, spending time in nature, healthy conversations and interactions with others..

And, sweat it out: Sweating is a great way for getting out toxins out of your system, to keep your immune system strong and have good blood flow, and to help balance emotions...

All come with incredible powers to grow in E.M. and keep all of your systems in awesome working order!

Arriving at some sort of Ending

"A story has no beginning or end: arbitrarily one chooses that moment of experience from which to look back or from which to look ahead..." – **Graham Greene**

All of this, what we can get out of it, who we are through it, our deepest nature, could this be the real answer that we're all looking for? Not a neat little formula on a chalk board, nor a blind devotion to religions or beliefs, of space conquests or advanced technologies, but through ourselves, the real nature of the universe, and of who we are within it. We become that which we seek above all else. Whoever God could be, we can only know through ourselves, whatever the fundamental nature of the universe, we can also only know through ourselves.

We are the truth, we are the reason, and we are the means. The only thing that remains, is to cast off the obstructions that stand in our way...

"Our human compassion binds us the one to the other – not in pity or patronizingly, but as human beings who have learnt how to turn our common suffering into hope for the future..."
– Nelson Mandela

For the Love of Yourself

Now, I hope I have brought some clarity as to why it can be so difficult at times to heal from our trauma and various internal dysfunctions and faulty programming, and why many people are not even aware of the extent they have. And also why it can look a lot like an inner reconciliation process, a full overhaul of your being, as not only do you need to reconcile your past and present experiences, but you also need to reconcile the various parts you have within yourself.

Yes, it can get discouraging, and yes sometimes with years of traditional therapy those deeper wounds might still not have surfaced. It takes time, and also requires some experimentation with various methods and systems. Journaling alone can help a lot, especially at first, and is easily accessible, but it is limited, like any one particular technique. Therapy with a proper health care professional can help a lot as well, but many therapists or psychologists limit their practice to certain techniques, and often that alone is not quite enough, even if good progress can be made. Some do dream work, others support groups, various therapies, reading good books on particular subjects of interest, and many other healing modalities. Take some time to figure out for yourself which works best, but take it easy. It is not a race, not a competition, treat yourself well, you deserve every bit of progress you realize.

Keep in mind that you are building your own best relationship with yourself, your own true love, you. When couples hit major roadblocks in their own relationships and feel the need to split up, they often cite **"irreconcilable differences"** as the main reason, and often that is exactly the case. For people, those that do not live their own best life, their purpose, you can say that they have reached that point with themselves, they have arrived at an impasse, their deepest dreams and desires have butted heads against whatever that person decided to make their life of. Either they have chosen a career that does not support the progress of their deepest desires, either they have settled for relationships that do not suit them, that are not complimentary, have chosen to focus on money, or sought power when they should have surrendered to a higher goal. Either or, they have moved closer and closer to reaching that point within themselves, their true life on one side, and the life they have settled for on the other, inching closer to the dreaded "irreconcilable differences" stage with their own better self, then hope becomes lost somewhere in the vast expanse between those two opposed realities. Many people die like that, having never reconciled their deepest desires with the life they settled for, and that is saddening.

It is a fear that a lot of people have, to die without knowing how good they could have been, not knowing their true potential, not having healed all of their unreconciled parts. I personally believe that we all come back until we can truly make our lives the best it can be, until we finally overcome our internal differences, until we heal all of our wounds, and become the best version of ourselves, to reach our full potential. Whatever greater reality you choose to believe in, follow that to the end, and make it all of what you can be.

So again, to heal the world, we must first heal ourselves, and in doing that, we become instruments of powerful change.

*"You must understand the whole of life, not just one part of it.
That is why you must read, that is why you must look at the
skies, why you must sing, dance and write poems, and suffer,
and understand, for all that is life..."*
– Jiddu Krishnamurti

Hmmm, this seems to be "*La Grande Finale*", at least for now.

And if all of this work serves to help you to become more present, to become more loving, more matched to your skills, to become more, *you*... Well, getting at the bottom of things, isn't that what we are all looking for anyway?

With little space left, I thought this would make for a great ending: **Sex!**

I thought that would grab your attention... They say that sex sells, but I didn't want to cheapen it in that way and have it front and center, big ads and sexy people, so I tucked it all the way in the furthest corners of the book. Well, seriously, I have not mentioned it anywhere else because, for one, I am by no means a sex therapist, and I didn't want to go into it that much because it can get very complicated, and also I feel it is a more personal matter for people to explore in their own way. Yet I felt I should say at least something about it, as it can drive us so much in life, and not only drive us, but can be quite indicative in regards to our internal state of affairs, affairs, get it? Yep, keeping up the *serious not so serious* tone all the way to the sweeter end;)

But, I will not linger into it, just a quick mention to keep in mind that often our repressed stuff gets expressed in our sexual habits, how we do it, or not do it, our desires and fantasies, even with ourselves... Our proclivities towards our bedroom activities, or other places of our choosing, can be real eye openers when considering how it all relates with who we are, and who we are not. A lot of the things we are afraid to face within us, our own issues with our image, our past, our wants, power or lack of... There is definitely a lot to learn in this area of our lives in relationship to our dysfunctions and history, and also in what we desire to experience, so keep this in mind, and you might want to check out other resources on this topic at some point in your journey. It can go a long way to explore yourself as you are getting to know the full you, learning your own vocabulary, and of showing some resilience for not shying away from any topic, political, environmental, big or small, personal or not, and yes, even sex.

All of it as an all-encompassing portrait that paints the story of a human being with a multitude of goals and desires, a complicated mass of energies with often the simplest of wants that even one well timed hug can make the most dreadful of worries melt away into the background as if they never existed. That is love, and that is us, if we dare to work towards that future.

"For me, becoming isn't about arriving somewhere or achieving a certain aim. I see it instead as forward motion, a means of evolving, a way to reach continuously toward a better self. The journey doesn't end..."
— **Michelle Obama**

Still with me?

Here's one last song to send you on your way to greater destinations:

MUSICAL INTERLUDE: One more for the road... ***Hold On***, by **The Brevet**

Take care...

Appendix and Resources

Here is a non-exhaustive list of books that I feel have greatly contributed to my life path, in no particular order:

Man's Search for Meaning, by Viktor E. Frankl
The Power of Now, by Eckhart Tolle
Anatomy of the Spirit, by Caroline Myss
The Untethered Soul, by Michael A. Singer
Complex PTSD: From Surviving to Thriving, by Pete Walker
The Seat of the Soul, by Gary Zukav
You Can Heal Your Life, by Louise Hay
The Alchemist, by Paulo Coelho
The Road Less Traveled, by M. Scott Peck, M.D.
Outwitting the Devil, by Napolean Hill
Siddhartha, by Hermann Hesse
The Body Keeps the Score, by Bessel Van Der Kolk
Adult Children of Emotionally Immature Parents, by Lindsay C. Gibson
The Art of Happiness, by the Dalai Lama and Howard Cutler
Essential Writings, by Thich Nhat Hanh
The Power of Intention, by Wayne W. Dyer
The Little Prince, by Antoine de Saint-Exupéry
The Gifts of Imperfection, by Brené Brown

ADDITIONAL RESOURCES:

"Compassion is not an option. It's the key to our survival..."
— **Karen Armstrong**

<u>Support groups and abuse prevention</u> (links might be subject to change)

ANXIETY AND DEPRESSION ASSOCIATION OF AMERICA
https://adaa.org/adaa-online-support-group
TOP PICKS LIST
https://www.verywellmind.com/best-online-anxiety-support-groups-4692353
HELP GUIDE
https://www.heretohelp.bc.ca/q-and-a/how-can-i-find-a-support-group
MENTAL HEALTH RESOURCES
https://nami.zendesk.com/hc/en-us/articles/360024615074-Are-there-any-online-resources-for-therapy-support-groups-or-mental-health-apps
CANADIAN WOMEN'S ASSOCIATION
https://canadianwomen.org/blog/warning-signs-abusive-relationship
END DOMESTIC ABUSE
https://www.enddomesticabuse.org/narcissistic_abuse.php

<u>Emotional and spiritual growth websites</u>

CHOPRA: https://chopra.com
INNER ENGINEERING: https://www.innerengineering.com
CHARTER FOR COMPASSION:
https://charterforcompassion.org
NATIONAL WELLNESS INSTITUTE:
https://nationalwellness.org
MIND TOOLS: https://www.mindtools.com

SEARCH INSIDE YOURSELF LEADERSHIP INSTITUTE:
https://siyli.org
MINDFUL: https://www.mindful.org
SIX SECONDS EQ NETWORK: https://www.6seconds.org
TONY ROBBINS: https://www.tonyrobbins.com
WHOLE BEING INSTITUTE:
https://wholebeinginstitute.com
GAIA: https://www.gaia.com
MINDSPACE: https://www.mindspacewellbeing.com
PICK THE BRAIN: https://www.pickthebrain.com
SELF GROWTH: https://www.selfgrowth.com

Body and Mind practices:

Yoga and Qigong: https://www.yoqi.com
Meditation and resources:
https://www.tarabrach.com/guided-meditations
Guided meditations:
https://www.audiodharma.org/series/1/talk/1835
The free mindfulness project:
http://www.freemindfulness.org/download
Brain FM: https://www.brain.fm
Positive Magazine Meditation on YouTube:
https://www.youtube.com/channel/UCFlcx_5HUbSh6hsl3Z
MKZkw
NY Times Meditation blog:
https://www.nytimes.com/topic/subject/meditation
Hay House YouTube:
https://www.youtube.com/channel/UCYTGWaEBUiCYhCESR
wu8loA
HeartMath Institute: https://www.heartmath.com

Apps, fairly self-explanatory

- Calm
- Headspace
- The Mindfulness App
- Buddhify
- Breethe
- Ten Percent Happier Meditation
- Smiling Mind
- Insight Timer
- Chopra
- Omvana

About the author:

Michael is an author, certified emotional intelligence practitioner and founder of *The E.Q. Revolution*, whose aims are of advocating for increased social responsibility through the positive transformation of individuals, emotional growth and maturity, and by the reduction of narcissistic and antisocial influences in our world...

Leading the way to a new era of kindness and compassionate way of life for humanity, the next big shift in our evolution.

"Without love, nothing is real, as all things that don't matter will eventually fade away back into the illusions they came from, and only the truth will stand mighty in the end..."

THE E.Q. REVOLUTION

From

Emotional Intelligence

To

Emotional Maturity

**<u>Please leave a review</u>: If you've enjoyed the read, believe in the message and got a few good things out of the book, then please write a review on Amazon (or where you got the book from) and/or invite people that you know who would be interested to get it for themselves, it is greatly appreciated.

You can help to give a boost to indie authors and an extra push to make this place of ours shine bright!

Thank you for purchasing this book

To receive special offers, bonus content,
and information on new releases and other material,
sign up for our newsletter:
"<u>newsletter@theeqrevolution.org</u>"

And visit our website:
"*<u>https://theeqrevolution.org</u>*"

Also, like us on **Facebook**, where you can find a lot more content, articles, and join a growing group of people interested in positive change, for themselves, and the world:
https://www.facebook.com/TheEQRevolution

Manufactured by Amazon.ca
Bolton, ON

24002359R00149